*The*
# MERCEDES-BENZ
*Story*

# The
# MERCEDES-BENZ
## Story

Louis William Steinwedel

*629.222
S†37m*

**CHILTON'S SEBRING SERIES**

Chilton Book Company

PHILADELPHIA • NEW YORK • LONDON

**1504115**

*William George Hudson*
AND
*Helen Hall Hudson*

# Acknowledgments

Through the years many people have contributed to the story of Mercedes-Benz. Many people have contributed also to the production of *The Mercedes-Benz Story*. Accordingly, the author would like to express his deep appreciation for the gracious assistance provided by Count Marcus Clary, Director of Special Programs, Mercedes-Benz of North America; Mr. Artur Keser, Head of Press Department, Daimler-Benz A.G., Stuttgart—Unterturkheim; Mr. Enzo Stuarti; Mr. "Skitch" Henderson; The Indianapolis Motor Speedway Corp.; Mr. Josef Riedlbauer for technical assistance; and Monsieur J. Fouquet, Le Secretaire General, Automobile Club de France.

*Louis William Steinwedel*

BALTIMORE, MARYLAND, 1969

# Contents

# The
# MERCEDES-BENZ
## Story

*Chapter* 1

# Daimler and Benz: The Invisible Partnership

Alexander King, the viper-tongued Viennese raconteur, once told a story about returning home to his native Austria after attaining some measure of success in America. As the local boy who made good, he was accosted by a wild-eyed inventor who dragged him up to a lonely Alpine chalet to show him "a marvellous new machine" which he was sure Alex could take back to America and with it make fortunes for both of them. With his impish smile King told his waiting audience that, "The poor fool had *re-invented* the typewriter."

In the same part of the world, over half a century earlier, Gottlieb Daimler and Karl Benz were *co-inventing* the automobile, each totally unaware of the other's efforts. The sixty miles separating Daimler in Cannstatt from Benz in Mannheim might as well have been an ocean. It seems one of the most curious coincidences of history that these two men, separately but almost simultaneously, solved the problems of creating the first practical motor vehicles powered by internal combustion engines. There had been other

Gottlieb Daimler 1834–1900. His memorials are the company that bears his name and the philosophy that each new car should be technically superior to its predecessor.

pioneers such as France's Etienne Lenoir and the Viennese Sigfried Marcus who ran a primitive *motorwagen* on the day on which the Civil War ended in America. But it is from Daimler's and Benz's original vehicles, which first ran in 1885, that the entire modern motorcar industry is descended.

Gottlieb Daimler's (properly pronounced Dime-ler) background and the prelude to the automobile do not merge at

all with the Hollywood-type image of the bright but informally educated young man who shuts himself up in a barn
and proceeds—after being duly misunderstood and laughed
at, of course—to astound the world with a brilliant inven-
tion. To the contrary, Daimler had about the best technical
education available, was a successful engineer with a pros-
perous company, and did not run his first motorcar until he
was more than fifty years old. Born into a fairly affluent
middle class family in Schorndorf in the Kingdom of Wurttemberg on the 17th of March, 1834, young Daimler's first
experience in creating things with metal came in the local
gunsmith's shop where he was apprenticed for four years.
His exposure to the theory and practice of engineering was
widened while he worked at a machine works in Alsace-
Lorraine, and formalized at the Stuttgart Polytechnic from
which he was graduated in 1859. Daimler's latent talent and
devotion to his profession were noticed by a wealthy and
intelligent man, Dr. Ferdinand Steinbeis. As his mentor,
Steinbeis suggested that some exposure to the ways of the
greatest industrial nation on earth, England, would be valuable to Daimler.

The young German engineer could not have found a better school than the great Whitworth works, a center of
science, manufacturing, and innovative engineering presided
over by a true Renaissance man totally dedicated to his
work, Sir Joseph Whitworth. At the time, Whitworth was
a leading armament builder, and one of his inventions must
have impressed the gunsmith's apprentice from Schorndorf,
a hexagonal-bore sharpshooter's rifle which was deadly accurate at over a mile range. It gives an interesting perspec-
tive to consider that at about the time Daimler was at Whitworth's, the firm was building advanced breechloading artillery used by the Confederate army to shell Union positions
at Gettysburg. Another curious angle is that the company

A brilliant engineer with an incisive mind, Wilhelm Maybach was associated with Gottlieb Daimler even before the days of the first automobile. Responsible for many of the company's triumphs, he was justly "the power beside the throne" at Daimler's.

would later build the famous Rudge wire wheels on which Daimler's Mercedes cars would race to glory.

During the next few years, Daimler pursued his study of European engineering centers, and later accepted a series of increasingly important appointments with German industrial firms. At the same time, he found a wife and started a family. Daimler had felt for some years that old-fashioned steam power must eventually give way to some form of internal combustion engine. In 1860, he had gone to Paris to examine Etienne Lenoir's stationary engine which ran on a gaseous fuel. Daimler was sure that an improved form of the internal combustion engine would someday come to something important, but he was unable to convince any of his employers that the firmly entrenched steam engine would ever be threatened by a little single cylinder engine that went "poof, poof".

Another German, Nikolaus August Otto, persevered with the four cycle stationary gas engine, brought it to a point of commercial perfection, and founded the Deutz Gas Motor Works. The new company was a forecast of things to come and in 1872 it hired Gottlieb Daimler as Chief Engineer and gave him *carte blanche*. One of his first acts was to bring in Wilhelm Maybach as Chief Designer, a man of technical brilliance equal to his own and who, perhaps even more than Daimler himself, was responsible for the original Mercedes car. In short, Daimler and his old friend Maybach labored long and hard for the Deutz Gas Motor Works and the firm prospered phenomenally. But success was not without friction between "management" and "research". Otto and his directors realized that they had saleable merchandise and wanted Daimler's impressive talent directed totally toward streamlining production, at which he had already been very successful. Daimler, on the other hand, was the classically curious scientist and wanted to experiment with more efficient, higher-speed engines. The rift widened and the break finally came in 1882 when Daimler withdrew from the firm after a decade of devotion to it.

Daimler moved to the pleasant little town of Cannstatt, installed his family in a comfortable house at number thirteen Taubenheimstrasse, and then retreated to a summerhouse-turned-workshop out back. On his usual dawn to midnight schedule and with Wilhelm Maybach lured away from Deutz, it took Daimler about a year to accomplish his first goal—a lightweight high speed, high efficiency, gas engine which he patented on the 16th of

Gottlieb Daimler's first motor vehicle, his single-cylinder motorcycle which first ran on 10th November, 1885. The jockey wheels retracted once the cycle was moving.

Daimler ordered this Victoria built by Wimft & Son, Stuttgart coachbuilders, and then powered it with his 1.5 horsepower single-cylinder engine in 1886. The finned radiator for the cooling system can be seen behind the rear seat.

December, 1883. A significant feature of Daimler's new engine was "hot tube ignition", the first simplified ignition system suitable for use on a motor vehicle. Previous combustion engines used a slide valve which opened to expose the explosive mixture in the cylinder to a flame, a system which could obviously produce only very low revolutions. Daimler's system used a platinum tube inserted through the cylinder wall, the exposed end of which was heated by an alcohol flame. Although primitive compared with electric ignition, it permitted an unheard of engine speed of nine hundred revolutions compared with less than two hundred RPM of other engines.

Within two years, Daimler had solved the problems of mounting a vertical version of his engine in the world's first motorcycle, fiitting it with an early float-type carburetor for more fully regulated fuel and air mixing, and transmitting power from the one half horsepower quarter litre engine to the rear wheel. On the 10th of November, 1885, the eldest Daimler son, Paul, drove the motorcycle from Cannstatt to the site of the present great Daimler-Benz plant at Unterturkheim. The test was an unqualified success and sent Daimler on to bigger things, this time with four wheels.

One of the bigger things was a specially altered twin seat Victoria carriage built by Wimft & Son, Stuttgart coachbuilders, into which Daimler installed a 1½-horsepower, one-cylinder engine (in the back seat). Power was transmitted to the rear wheels by different-size belt pulleys, according to various ratios. There was an interesting and effective water-cooled heat-dispersing system with a finned radiator just behind the rear seat. Despite some natural early suspicions, mechanical-minded Germans took to Daimler's plans to motorize their quiet little Nineteenth Century world, with relatively good humour. Certainly they accepted the infant motorcar better than people in England where, up to 1896, self-powered vehicles could not legally exceed four miles per hour (two in town areas) and had to be preceded by a man carrying a red flag. Enthusiastically, Daimler rushed ahead to adapt his engines to boats, trolley cars, narrow gauge trains, fire engines, and even an airship. It is interesting to consider that as early as 1888 you could arrive at the Stuttgart railway station and hail a Daimler motor taxi, the world's first.

The widespread application of Daimler's engines on road, rail, and water was encouraging and a Daimler engine in the air was a forecast of things to come. In 1887, Daimler invited the dirigible builder Dr. Karl Wolfert to try a specially built two horsepower engine to power the propellers of his airship. The doctor was delighted at finding a light-weight and efficient engine suitable for air travel and a test was conducted on a summer Sunday afternoon, 12th August, 1888, in which the airship took off, made a 2½ mile controlled powered flight, and landed gently. On that day Daimler's engine became the first internal combustion engine to power an aircraft in flight.

By the end of the 1880s, Gottlieb Daimler found himself with a factory at number 67 Ludwigstrasse, home of the dynamically successfully new Daimler Motoren Gesellschaft. He had entered the decade a disgruntled employee of the Deutz Gas Motor Works and finished it with a promising business of his own that left Deutz in the backwash. Had he been endowed with August Otto's conservatism, he could easily have devoted the rest of his life to casually perfecting his existing engines, and growing fat on profits, "bratwurst und bier." The sale of marine engines alone had been fantastically successful; many commercial firms, the German Navy, harbor police, and even Bismarck himself used Daimler powered motorboats, and Daimler had his own shipyard for building motor tugs. But the businessman flush with success did not lose the touch of the idealistic scientist who wanted more than anything to build good motorcars, and then *better* motorcars.

With Maybach at his side, Daimler spent long hours in the workshop and early in 1889 came up with a revolutionary vehicle. This time, he conceived of the motorcar as an independent entity, not merely as a motorized carriage. The new twin cylinder V-type engine (which amazingly cut the power-to-weight ratio by one half) formed an integral unit with the tubular steel chassis. Quite ingeniously, the cooling liquid was pumped through the tubular chassis structure which doubled as a radiator. Nearly half a century later, Dr.

Ferdinand Porsche would adapt the same chassis-cooling concept to help cool his rear-engined Auto-Union racers of the 1930s, and the idea has been used on subsequent racing cars. The new Daimler car had a four-speed gear change, with ratios providing for speeds of 2.5 MPH in first, 4.5 MPH in second, 6.5 MPH in third, and 11 MPH in top gear. Exhibited at the Paris Exhibition of 1889, the Daimler "wire wheel" car caused a sensation and the French firms of Peugeot and Panhard & Levassor hurried to place orders for Daimler engines for their cars. At about the same time, similar negotiations were going on with the American piano

Daimler's "wire wheel" car of 1889 was his first expression of the motorcar as an independent entity, rather than as a "motorized carriage." It featured a twin cylinder V-engine designed as an integral unit with the steel tubular chassis, which cleverly carried the cooling fluid.

Karl Benz 1844–1929. With Daimler, Benz shares the title of the father of the modern motor car. His very first car, which ran early in 1885, was a remarkably advanced answer to the challenge of internal combustion locomotion.

maker William Steinway who obtained the Daimler franchise in America and brought Daimler to the U.S. in 1891 to demonstrate his cars and engines at the Columbian Exposition in Chicago.

By 1892, the motorcar business was on the verge of becoming big business and with it came corporate complexities to confound Daimler and his endless research. Daimler Motoren Gesellschaft executives were singing a song long familiar to Daimler; push production at the expense of development. When the tune became too loud, Daimler and Maybach, as they had done at Deutz, left the firm and set up a quiet workshop to continue developing the automobile. The work proved valuable; Daimler and Maybach developed an efficient, quiet-running, belt-driven car and made use of a new float-type carburetor.

Meanwhile, DMG found Daimler not so dispensable as they thought; during his absence of three years they sold only a dozen cars. However, one of them was the first recorded sale of an automobile to reigning royalty, a surrey-type of vehicle purveyed to the Sultan of Morocco, whose descendants incidentally are still loyal to Daimler-Benz cars. Without Daimler at the helm of DMG, other pioneers were forging ahead and the axe fell at the famous Paris-Rouen trials on 22nd June, 1894, the world's first automobile "race". Although the first four gas-engine-powered cars over the finish line were driven by Daimler engines, they were embarrassingly mounted in Panhard and Peugeot cars! In the first motor race held in America, in Chicago in 1895, a Benz car won. Fortunately, a rapprochement was effected between Daimler and DMG with Daimler as Chairman of the Board and Wilhelm Maybach as Technical Director. It was fortunate for the firm and for the history of the automobile, because momentous days were just ahead.

In addition to growing French and Italian competition, Daimler's great rival lay only about sixty miles away in Mannheim behind the impressive sounding title of "Benz und Cie; Rheinische Gasmotorenfabrik". The road to the motorcar had been a rougher one for Karl Benz than even for Gottlieb Daimler. A mishap with an earlier form of motorized transport, the locomotive, deprived Benz of his father when the boy was two and his young mother struggled heroically to see him educated. Like Daimler, he followed theory with practice in the form of hard labor at various industrial firms in the Karlsruhe area. Unlike Daimler, he lacked the means for junkets to inspect foreign engi-

Benz's original car, which first ran in 1885, was a remarkably advanced machine for a first attempt. From the beginning, Benz saw the motorcar as a total concept rather than as a "motorized buggy," and his first car incorporated such features as electric ignition, effective throttle control, mechanical valves, horizontal flywheel, and even a comfortably upholstered seat. In tests through 1886 Benz developed the car to deliver a reliable 9 MPH. (*Courtesy, Daimler-Benz*)

neering showpieces, and financial problems were constant companions in his efforts to develop his first motorcar.

In his twenties Benz had worked for a carriage builder in Stuttgart, but by 1877 he was at work designing a two-stroke gas engine, and later became involved in a modest stationary gas engine enterprise, the "Gasmotorenfabrik Mannheim A.G.". The combination of the two, vehicles and gas engines, seemed a natural step to Benz and his burning desire was to create a practical self-propelled vehicle. But, just as Daimler had not seen eye to eye with the Deutz works, so Benz had a turbulent (and much shorter) career with the Mannheim Gas Motor Works and left it in 1883 to form Benz und Cie; Rheinische Gasmotorenfabrik with the help of outside capital. It was this new organization which finally gave him the resources and a breathing spell to pull his ideas together and build his first car.

Benz's perseverance with the two-stroke engine (he perfected it to a higher degree than anyone else) gave him valuable background in developing a four-stroke engine for his first vehicle. Even before he started he had an effective throttle control arrangement and an advanced electric ignition system which, of course, was eventually to displace Daimler's "hot tube" ignition. Benz made his first trials in 1885 of a car which was an astonishingly advanced machine for a first attempt, in some ways quite superior to Daimler's first and even second efforts. Benz leaped ahead of the motorized buggy stage and his car was closer in concept to Daimler's model of 1889. It was a tiller-steered three-wheeler with two, big, spidery, rubber-rimmed wire wheels at the rear which lent a sort of primitive elegance.

The single cylinder 2/3 horsepower engine mounted just behind the upholstered seat was a carefully thought out piece of machinery. In addition to the Benz throttle and electric ignition innovations, the motor used mechanically operated slide-type inlet valves and poppet exhaust valves, resulting in good efficiency. To counteract centrifugal force created by the flywheel, Benz mounted it horizontally, which helped simplify cornering. Power transmission was accomplished by a pulley and belt drive to a true differential gear and from that point power was conveyed to the rear driving wheels by side chains.

Through 1885, Benz adjusted, upgraded, and revised his car and took it for longer, more re-assuring runs. By the 3rd of July, 1886, he was satisfied to expose it to public gaze for the first time and took it out onto the streets of Mannheim where it naturally caused great commotion. A few years later (as recorded by Currier & Ives) American experimenters frightened domestic horses and delighted local children with horseless carriages copied from Karl Benz. More public runs followed and almost with each one reliability increased and speeds of nine miles an hour were produced.

As a result of his trials, Karl Benz received notoriety, congratulations, some speculations about his sanity, a few glowing press notices, and precious few buyers for the "Patent Motor-Wagen Benz". There were many lookers but few takers. The image of the infant automobile was not particularly helped when one of the earliest Benz buyers was shortly afterward committed to an insane asylum, presumably for other reasons.

However, with financial re-organization of Benz und Cie and the growing sale of his stationary gas engines to pay the way, Benz continued to experiment and perfect his automobile designs. His next major breakthrough came in 1891 in the form of a new four-wheel car which he called the "Victoria"; named for "the victory of a happy idea" as he quaintly phrased it.

The Victoria, which prophetically was the first car ever to bear a girl's name, was a quite different machine from Benz's light wire wheeler of 1885/86. Benz intended the Victoria as a reliable and luxurious touring car and fitted it with a series of increasingly powerful three to six-horsepower engines to meet the demands made on it. The new Benz also boasted some important technical improvements including poppet valves, float feed carburetor, timing adjustment, and a control to regulate the mixture being fed into the cylinder which increased engine efficiency. The Benz Victoria offered comfort, speeds of up to 20 MPH, and a good degree of long distance reliability; in effect, it

Benz's second car, called the Victoria, represented the germ of the Grand Touring car by offering performance, comfort, and long distance reliability. (*Courtesy, Daimler-Benz*)

was the first Grand Touring car. In the summer of 1894, a wealthy Austrian named Theodor Von Liebieg drove a Victoria nearly six hundred miles across Germany and France and opened a new era by pioneering what he called "The discovery of the countryside by means of the automobile."

The Victoria was necessarily an expensive car and, even though Benz was finding more customers for his cars (even royal patronage from the King of Belgium), he realized that a cheap, simple car would be necessary to carry the automobile to the general public. Using the technical advances of the Victoria as a model, Benz designed a small, light car that was to become a landmark in automotive history. Although mass-production was left to Henry Ford, the Benz Velo was the world's first series-produced car. A year later, the little Velo was the most popular car in the Benz catalogue; the Daimler-Benz archives record that 134 Benzes were built in 1895 and 62 of them were Velos.

Benz und Cie flourished through the carefree Nineties and more models were added to the line; the "Phaeton", the "Comfortable" (a revised Velo), the "Dos-a-Dos", the "Vis-a-Vis", the "Mylord", the "Spider", the "Tonneau", the "Duc", the "Break", and the "Ideal" (another attempt at an

Benz's daughter, Clara, at the controls of a Velo. The Benz women were actively involved in automobiles. Bertha Benz once piled her two young sons into her husband's first car and, unknown to him, took off on a long distance trip to become the world's first woman driver. (*Courtesy, Daimler-Benz*)

A Benz Velo of 1894; the world's first series production automobile and the first attempt to put the motorcar within the reach of the general public. A sort of primeval Volkswagen, the Velo was simple, durable, and reliable. (*Courtesy, Daimler-Benz*)

inexpensive car). It was a rewarding and satisfying time for Benz, whose organization and production had leaped ahead of Daimler's. During the 1890s, Karl Benz became the world's pre-eminent motorcar manufacturer, with sales agencies in such removed capitals as Capetown, Mexico City, Buenos Aires, and Singapore. By the end of the decade he had built 2000 cars in all and had a production capacity of nearly 600 cars a year.

There was one thing, however, that Karl Benz was not usually willing to give his customers and that was speed. Benz himself was a courteous and careful driver with precise road manners and saw little point in tearing over primitive highways, even to impress potential buyers. However,

Daimler Phaeton of 1898 fitted with the early two-cylinder front mounted "Phoenix" engine producing 6 HP. Emil Jellinek owned a similar car as his first Daimler which served to whet his interest in the Daimler enterprise. (*Courtesy, Daimler-Benz*)

The 23 HP, four-cylinder Daimler "Phoenix" high performance car was partly coaxed into existence by Emil Jellinek and his demands for faster cars. The Phoenix was mechanically advanced but too fast for its short wheelbase and high center of gravity. (*Courtesy, Daimler-Benz*)

there is a delightful story that he made at least one exception to his philosophy. At the time, there was a four miles-per-hour speed limit in effect which even Benz considered conservative. He had invited the provincial minister to visit the Mannheim factory and sent a chauffeured car for the visiting officials. Along the way, officialdom was piqued to be passed by a milk wagon and asked the driver if he could step it up a bit. Obligingly, he blasted by the milk cart at four times the prescribed limit, to the delight of the minister who promptly failed to see the continued need for a speed limit. Titillated by the sensation of raw power, he had also failed to guess that the milk wagon was not there entirely by chance.

A little more such insight into human nature would perhaps have saved Benz some tense moments around the turn of the century. Balancing his brilliant inventive ability, Benz was endowed with a stolid, Teutonic conservatism, and his great success had temporarily turned his mind toward refining his original concepts instead of reaching out for new ideas, as Daimler and Maybach were doing. He was also quite reticent about racing, which even in the 1890s was beginning to influence automotive design. By the end of the Nineteenth Century Benz's single and double cylinder verged on the obsolete in comparison, for instance, with Daimler's new four cylinder "Phoenix" high performance car. Some considerable new thinking had to be done at Mannheim. It was, and a few years later the fastest car on earth was to be a Benz.

# Chapter 2

# The Mercedes is Born

The 1890s were exciting and effervescent years for the automobile. During this decade people began to cast off their suspicions and inhibitions—psychological and legal —about the new machines on their roads. In 1896, England repealed its infamous "Red Flag Law" requiring a man with a red flag to walk ahead of a car. Pioneer motorists celebrated with a joyous, if confused, "Emancipation Run" over the fifty miles between London and the seaside resort of Brighton. One of the thirty-three participants, Gottlieb Daimler, had reason to be especially delighted, and reflective. The "Brighton Run" survives today, with more pomp and pageantry than competition. In 1968, Prince Rainier of Monaco finished the run in a 1903 De Dion Bouton to receive a bronze medal decorated with a winged Mercury and the Britishly understated inscription, "For Punctual Arrival".

In the nineties the best engineering minds in Europe and America began to turn their attention to the automobile, and a lively debate developed over what was the best motive power for cars—internal combustion, steam, or electricity. Each school had its supporters and could point to some moment of triumph. With pioneers such as George Bouton perfecting fairly practical steam cars in the seventies and eighties, the steamers had seniority. In fact, it was a Bouton-built "steam tractor" that finished first in the 1894 Paris-Rouen, but the officials decided to give it second prize even though it had been first to finish. To further complicate things, they also split the first prize money and glory between Armand Peugeot's Daimler-engined car (which was second to finish) and a Daimler-engined Panhard (third). The French can be very amusing people when they put their minds to it.

The electric fanciers pointed to the smooth silence of their cars, and seldom mentioned things like battery re-charging and the short travel radius. They did, however, hasten to point out that before the close of the century Camille Jenatzy had driven a Jeantaud electric racing car—called *La Jamais Contente*—at the astonishing speed of 65 MPH.

Steam supporters hung on stubbornly; in America the Doble steam car was built into the 1930s and in 1906 a Stanley was supposed to have hit 197 MPH before it disintegrated across Daytona Beach. But the internal combustion engines of Daimler and Benz were the wave of the future. The handwriting was on the wall as early as the 1895 Paris-Bordeaux race. For nearly forty-nine solid hours, Emile Levassor pushed his Daimler-engined Panhard through the beautiful chateaux country of the Loire Valley to cover 745 miles non-stop and without serious incident. It was a singular triumph for the reliability of Daimler's engines (the next three cars also used them), and for Levassor a feat of heroic endurance to rank with Caracciola in the 1931 Mille Miglia and Sterling Moss on the same course in 1955.

In 1897 Daimler, despite failing health, was hard at work with Maybach on a new car called the "Phoenix" which moved the engine out from under (or behind) the seat and put it where it is usually found today, in front of the driver. This 1.5 litre machine moved one step further out of the carriage age by adopting an iron frame of U-beams and, on later models, pneumatic tires. But most significant was Daimler's growing concern about an efficient cooling system, a pre-requisite for anything purporting to be a high performance car. On the Phoenix he came up with the idea of placing a fan behind the radiator to increase the air flow, and thus decreased the amount of cooling water needed.

It was at this point in time that Emil Jellinek, one of the most colorful, influential, and perhaps least understood figures in early motoring history, appeared on the scene. His first contact with the Daimler Motoren Gesellschaft was characteristic of others that followed in his dozen or so years of association with it; he requested—pointedly—a car which would go faster than his new 6 HP "Phaeton" with the original two-cylinder Phoenix engine. Unencumbered by Karl Benz's reluctance about speed, Daimler and Maybach were working along that line and promptly replied to the effusive Mr. Jellinek's demands with a much souped-up four-cylinder 23/28 HP version of the Phoenix which was little less than an all-out racing machine. Jellinek was delighted, promptly ordered four cars, and entered the 1899 "Tour de Nice" which he won. Two cars were also entered in the La Turbie hill climb, near Nice, to be held on the 30th of March, 1900.

The new four-cylinder Phoenix represented something of an anomaly. Despite its mechanical superiority and the brilliant new engine which abundantly provided the raw speed Jellinek demanded, the Phoenix was a high, somewhat cumbersome car of short wheelbase. It quite flagrantly violated

Emil Jellinek, the motor-minded Austro-Hungarian Consul-General, banker, and businessman. His catalytic personality was instrumental to the success of Mercedes. (*Courtesy, Daimler-Benz*)

the modern Daimler-Benz philosophy that "the chassis should be faster than the engine." The point was tragically proved at La Turbie when Daimler's crack driver, Wilhelm Bauer, fatally crashed into the side of a mountain at the Grand Corniche curve. Nevertheless, the powerful new

Daimler attracted a great deal of attention, and the motor-minded American millionaire, Willie K. Vanderbilt, bought one to try on the good roads of Long Island. A few of his friends also bought expensive European cars, and the inevitable race came in early autumn of 1900 at Newport. When the dust settled, Vanderbilt had run the five-mile course in just under nine minutes and found himself the holder of something called "The Championship of America". Although no one had much idea what that ostentatious title meant, at least it marked the beginning of a long and durable friendship between Willie K. and the big German cars.

Jellinek was set back by the accident at La Turbie but not discouraged. In fact, he immediately entered into an agreement with DMG to purchase ten cars for re-sale on the Riviera. Up to this time, his enthusiasm for Daimler cars had made him the firm's best customer, purchasing some thirty-four cars most of which he re-sold at handsome profits. Emil Jellinek was then a director of the great French banking house, the Credit Lyonnais, a successful businessman and entrepreneur, and the Austro-Hungarian Consul-General at Nice—a sinecure that served mainly to cover his chest with an effulgent assortment of medals. He was a man of almost Latin passion (much of it directed at automobiles), colossal impatience, enormous self-confidence, and minute modesty. An incisive, and not altogether complimentary, biography, *My Father, Mr. Mercedes*, has lately been written by his son Guy Jellinek-Mercedes which offers an interesting glimpse into fin-du-siecle high life and Jellinek's catalytic effect on Mercedes cars.

Jellinek was, however, a decisive man who knew what he wanted and how to get it. And what he wanted from DMG was a car which was mechanically sophisticated, reliable, and—above all—fast. To get it, he now dealt with Daimler's son Paul and Wilhelm Maybach. (Gottlieb Daimler's obsession with work had finally caught up with him and he had died on the 6th of March, 1900.) Paul Daimler was then working on a smaller, somewhat refined 8 HP version of the Phoenix which featured a radical "honeycomb" radiator with a fan behind it, a new throttle control device, jet carburetor, and magneto ignition. The car fitted Jellinek's mental picture perfectly, except for the power which the Phoenix engine concepts could provide. Jellinek and *chef-konstructor* Maybach reasoned together over the proposed new high performance car, with Jellinek unabashedly making suggestions and directions to the greatest auto engineer alive. The Consul-General of the august Austro-Hungarian Empire was as thrilled as a three-year-old on Christmas, and happily agreed to underwrite work on the new car by ordering thirty-six of them at a cost of over half a million German marks. Besides the salutory effect on his chronic hypochondria, Jellinek also received as part of the agreement the sales rights for the new car in Austria, Hungary, France, Belgium, and America—and the concession that the car would be named "Mercedes" for his ten-year-old daughter.

Work was pushed hard on "Project Mercedes" through the winter of 1900/1901, for Jellinek was anxious to enter the new car in the Grand Prix of Pau, a 200-mile race to be run on the 17th of February, 1901, in southern France. Maybach was against it because the car had not been thoroughly tested, but Jellinek insisted and the first Mercedes was put on a train headed out of the German winter into the sunshine of the south of France. Lorraine Barrow, an accomplished driver who was killed driving a De Dietrich racing car in the bloody Paris-Madrid race two years later, was selected to drive the original Mercedes. At the race, Maybach's conservatism prevailed embarrassingly over

Emil Jellinek's daughter, Mercedes, for whom her father had the new Daimler car of 1900/1901 named. She was ten years old at the time. (*Courtesy, Daimler-Benz*)

Jellinek's enthusiasm; the newly designed clutch wouldn't hold, the gear shift jammed up tight, and Jellinek's pride and joy was left standing sad and lonely in the clouds of dust and exhaust at the start.

Maybach had the Mercedes team of six cars ready for the great Nice Speed Week held the 25th to 29th of March,

1901, and he was ready with a car which could truly be called revolutionary; it was an automobile that would influence others for years to come. The 5.9 litre engine with aluminum crankcase and cylinder block and a head in a single casting was a futuristic prediction. Inlet and exhaust valves were mechanically operated to attain a new level of engine efficiency, assisted by a centrifugal governor which could be adjusted by a hand-lever to give engine speeds between 300 and 1000 RPM. There was a pair of advanced jet carburetors (one for each pair of cylinders) and new low-tension magneto ignition by Bosch. Growing out of the base of the steering column—which was for the first time rakishly angled into the driver's lap—was a gear shift lever which, as Englishmen are fond of saying, fell easily to hand. It was a convenient, modern arrangement; and the shift lever connected to a four speed gate-type gear change which was superior to anything else in use at the time.

The innovation went further—from the modern pressed Krupp steel frame (some other builders continued to use wooden frames for several years) to the marvelous new honeycomb radiator with exactly 8070 cooling passages. The new radiator caused quite a sensation when news of it hit the motoring world; it was the last word in cooling systems, being able to cool the big 5.9 litre engine more effectively with about 2½ gallons of water than other cars could with smaller engines and ten-gallon cooling systems. From the front, the radiator offered a facade of neat little squares, vaguely suggestive of the compartmented Teutonic mind which had conceived it. The basic neat appearance of the radiator on this first Mercedes has been carried down through the years and is still easily recognized on current production cars.

With a few more new ideas thrown in for good measure, such as the Daimler-patent coil spring clutch, gearlock

The original 35 H.P. Mercedes of 1901 fitted as a two-seater competition car of the type

A memorable moment of glory; Wilhelm Werner at the wheel of Baron Rothschild's Mercedes after winning the 244-mile Nice distance race. The next car came in 26 minutes later. (*Courtesy, Daimler-Benz*)

brake fitted to the transmission, and improved internal expanding brakes on the rear wheels, the new Mercedes was literally light years ahead of any other car on the road. Some idea of its status can be gained by comparing it with Daimler's original Phoenix car of only four years earlier. This car, which was advanced in 1897, weighed more than the new Mercedes, put out only 6 HP, and had a top speed of about 26 MPH. The Mercedes had a German horsepower rating of 35, a top speed of nearly 60 MPH, and a power to weight ratio of 14.9 pounds per horsepower which was not approached by other makers for a long time. As a total concept, the Mercedes represented the first modern automobile. Of all those who were moved to superlatives about the new Daimler car, perhaps the most discerning was Paul Meyan, Secretary-General of the influential Automobile Club de France, who observed that "We have entered the age of the Mercedes," which was probably not an easy thing for a loyal, auto-minded Frenchman to say.

Today, Nice is a quiet crystal, red velvet, and rococo backwater customarily frequented by retired English civil servants and a few Americans who have discovered that their nouvelle francs last a little longer there. But in 1901 Nice was very different, a sort of high collar Edwardian St. Tropez or Cap Ferrat, if those two concepts can co-exist without curdling. And what was happening in Nice in Emil Jellinek's day was Speed Week, a glittering gala devoted to racing, betting on, looking at, and being seen in society's newest toy, the automobile. The program for Speed Week included events run for record, distance, and hill climbing ability, and included "sports" and "touring cars" categories open to both professional and amateur "gentlemen drivers". Unfortunately for motor fans, nothing quite comparable survives today.

The first event at Nice was the distance race from Nice

to Aix to Sénas to Salon and back to Nice through 244 miles of spectacular mountain scenery. Three Mercedes were entered, but eyes and odds were on the one handled by Daimler's top driver, Wilhelm Werner. Mysteriously entered under the name "Dr. Pascal", the car actually belonged to Baron Henri de Rothschild of the famous banking family. By using a fictitious *nom de guerre*, Rothschild bowed to the lingering prejudice that playing with automobiles was something less than an aristocratic pastime, although he did drive personally in four Speed Week events. Jellinek himself had used the same subterfuge in earlier races, entering under the name "Monsieur Mercedes". Werner blasted the Baron's car through the mountains with marvelous aplomb and returned to Nice in 6 hours and 45 minutes, 26 minutes ahead of his nearest rival.

As the week wore on, Mercedes cars continued to take first prizes and set records with remarkable regularity. Again on Baron Rothschild's car, Werner took the "Mile Race of Nice" in both the standing start category and for the flying kilometer. Later, he triumphed again in the treacherous La Turbie hill climb, with another Mercedes only a few seconds behind him. Lorraine Barrow was nicely compensated for his embarrassment at Pau the month before on the unprepared Mercedes by establishing a new world's record for the standing start mile on an internal combustion car. Everyone connected with the venture was delighted, but none more than Emil Jellinek who envisioned waiting lines of the wealthy queueing up to buy the three dozen Mercedes cars which he had on order. But, doubtless, he was even more elated over the obvious vindication of his judgment and faith in the Mercedes. The day after it was all over he is supposed to have said to Paul Meyan, "That car will be as nothing beside what you will see next year." And he was right.

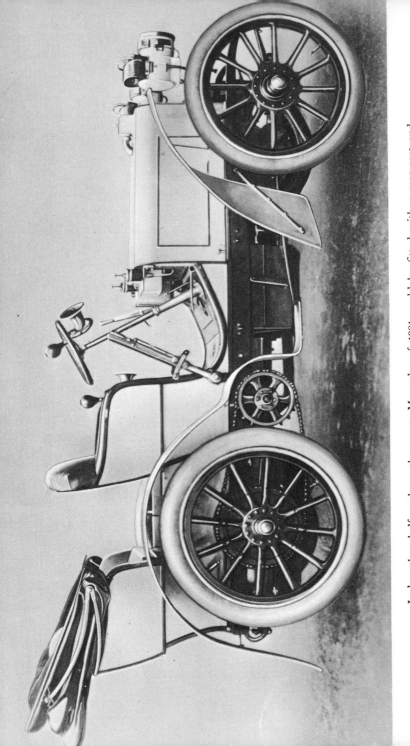

In less than half an hour the sports Mercedes of 1901 could be fitted with a rear seat and landau top to become a sedate and elegant touring car. (*Courtesy, Daimler-Benz*)

A two-cylinder, 16 HP Benz racing car of 1900, adequate for the time but soon to be overshadowed by the emerging Mercedes. (*Courtesy, Daimler-Benz*)

The Mercedes car of 1902 was generally called the 40 HP model because Maybach, in addition to cutting 117 pounds off the engine weight, had again managed to increase efficiency by further improvements in regulating the air-fuel mixture. Also, by synchronizing the inlet and exhaust valves, he brought an unheard of smoothness and silence to the internal combustion engine. New ignition was added, the radiator fan improved, and the cooling system capacity reduced from nine to seven litres. As Emil Jellinek had predicted, 1902 at Nice was gilding the lily. The 40 HP again played the all-conquering hero of the Riviera, and shortly afterward Baron De Caters did the flying kilometer in a 40 HP at 75 MPH. The Mercedes had safely arrived as "the" car for both sports and touring and DMG's order

Basing the "Sixty" Mercedes of 1903 on a large 60 HP touring car, Wilhelm Maybach laid a 9.2 litre engine into a chassis which was stronger but over 200 pounds lighter than the 40 HP Mercedes of 1902. Among other novelties the "Sixty" had water-cooled brakes. (*Courtesy, Daimler-Benz*)

books were bulging. One of their semi-satisfied customers was King Leopold of Belgium, a full fledged member of Jellinek's exploding cult of speed. Cornering Wilhelm Maybach at the Fifth Annual Paris Salon in December of 1902, the King had praise for the 40 HP which he already owned but, like Jellinek, pressed for something faster. "Unless I can touch 80 MPH, it is no use to me", he told Maybach. Daimler's Chief engineer went into a little explanation of automotive engineering basics and then, with good reason, suggested a little more patience.

In 1903, came the famous Mercedes "Sixty", one of the epic cars of all time. Maybach developed the "Sixty" out of the bigger engined 60 HP touring model, fitting the big 9.2 litre engine into a strengthened chassis which he simultaneously lightened by over two hundred pounds. The new Sixty preserved all the virtues of the previous 40 HP, and added some tasty new ones of its own, such as interchangeable sprockets for the chain drive which could be varied according to track conditions, double ignition, an improved honeycomb radiator with double the cooling surface, new suspension, new starter, and a curious little gadget which spritzed water on the brake drums every time you hit the brake pedal. In a sense, the Sixty was a statement of its era, a summing up of the Daimler-Maybach expertise in building high performance machinery. Meteorically it rose to become the ultimate status symbol of its day, and no self-respecting millionaire under the age of fifty dared be without one. David Scott-Moncrief, the eminent British motoring writer, called it "the beau ideal of Edwardian youth." Visually, the Sixty was a very appealing car, resplendent in German racing white, meticulously buffed brass, and with carefully polished artillery wheels. It was a business-like machine with nothing laid on for effect, and its purely functional elegance linked it in blood line with such distant descendants as the SSK and 300 SLR.

Naturally the newest Mercedes was at Nice in the Spring of 1903 to uphold its intransigent tradition there. The distance race was again added to the voluminous Daimler record books, which have recorded every Daimler success since the Paris-Rouen of 1894. New records were also set for the standing mile and the La Turbie hill climb. A new average speed record of 74.3 MPH was also established at Nice that year with a Sixty Mercedes owned by an Englishman named Alfred Harmsworth, later Lord Northcliffe. The carefully preserved car has stayed in the Harmsworth family for all the intervening years and today resides comfortably in Lord Montagu's motor museum at Beaulieu.

But whatever glory was gained by Mercedes that year at Nice was clouded over by the death of Count Eliot Zborowski, one of the most colorful personalities of early motor racing. Zborowski was an intensely interesting individual, and probably the prototype of all noble born Europeans who have devoted considerable portions of their lives and fortunes to exciting automobiles. Parenthetically, it was originally his idea that competition cars of different countries should have their own national racing color. Having practically—but not technically—won the 1902 Paris-Vienna race in a Mercedes, Zborowski was no stranger to Daimler's cars and had entered his big, white Sixty in the La Turbie hill climb. The stories as to what actually happened vary, but one has it that one of his cuff links caught in the column mounted throttle control, causing him to accelerate into a turn. The car crashed. The remainder of the events was cancelled, but the Zborowski tradition was carried on by his son, Count Louis. His career, which produced the famous Mercedes-based "Chitty-Bang-Bang" cars, was capped with perhaps the weirdest and most inexplicable incident in all motoring history, and more will be said about him later.

It did not take long for the Sixty to grow again, this time to the great Ninety. The Ninety was an epically conceived venture but one which seemed destined to be dogged by bad luck. A half dozen of the monsters were ready to run in the much promoted Paris-Madrid race of 1903, which degenerated into a debacle of death and disaster mainly because no one made much effort to keep spectators out of the way of cars moving at 80 to 90 MPH speeds. French officials were horrified at the rate at which drivers were splattering themselves, their riding mechanics, livestock, and the general population over the landscape, and stopped the race at Bordeaux. They decreed that the surviving cars be sent back to Paris by train and would not even trust the drivers to drive them to the railroad station, ordering the cars dragged in by draft horses. A good bet to win the Paris-Madrid had been the red-bearded Belgian firebrand Camille

Jenatzy in a new Ninety, but not long after the start his performance became spotty. Jenatzy pulled over and his mechanic scrambled into the carburetor and came up with a big fat horsefly which had effectively laid low this great twelve litre machine.

In 1899, James Gordon Bennett, the American newspaper publisher, decided that the cause of motoring would be helped by a great annual international automobile race. So, he had Tiffany's whip up a seventy-pound silver trophy and, with a string of newspapers including the Paris edition of the New York Herald to provide the publicity, he was in business. The first three Gordon Bennett events were run concurrently with other races and were somewhat low key. The first, in 1900, was part of the Paris-Lyon; the second was combined with the 1901 Paris-Bordeaux; and the third was part of the great 1902 Paris-Vienna with the Gordon Bennett part ending at Innsbruck. This one was an upset, won by a very courageous Englishman named Selwyn Edge on a longshot Napier car. Under the Bennett rules, Britain became the host nation for 1903, a somewhat embarrassing situation because after the Paris-Madrid sensation racing was about as acceptable in Britain as pawning the crown jewels. This was circumvented by transferring the race to Ballyshannon, Ireland, possibly on the theory that Irishmen were more expendable.

While DMG was readying a team of five Nineties for the Gordon Bennett on the 2nd of July, fire leveled the factory at Cannstatt on the 10th of June and hardly left one brick standing on another. The sole surviving Ninety was on the high seas bound for America and Willie K. Vanderbilt in Daytona Beach where he set a 92.3 MPH world's record with it. Undaunted, Daimler borrowed a Sixty from one of their wealthy American clients, Clarence Dinsmore (with Emil Jellinek as intermediary) and signed Camille Jenatzy

When a fire at the Daimler plant destroyed five "Nineties" entered in the Gordon Bennett race in Ireland, Camille Jenatzy was put on a borrowed "Sixty" and proceeded to win with an epic, daring drive at speeds up to 85 MPH. (*Courtesy, Daimler-Benz*)

to drive it. Meanwhile, they bought land at nearby Unter-turkheim and began a new factory on the site of the present one.

On the appointed field of honor Jenatzy found formid-able competition lurking in the Irish morning mists. There was Edge on a big 13 litre Napier, a pair of reputable French Panhards displacing some 13.7 litres apiece, and there was even a trio of American entries—a Peerless and a pair of Wintons, one a 17 litre! With the U.S. cars in the running, Jenatzy must have been puzzled to see Dinsmore, the owner of the car under him, distributing miniature American flags to the drivers as souvenirs.

Although it has been alleged that Jenatzy's Sixty had its 9.2 litre engine replaced with the twelve litre Ninety en-gine, it is hard to imagine how this could have been done in view of the destruction at Cannstatt. With the 9.2 litre engine, Jenatzy's Mercedes was actually one of the smallest cars in the race in that age of giants; only the smaller Win-ton and two 45 HP Napiers had less displacement. How-ever, the Mercedes had the edge on suspension, maneuver-ability and response, and Jenatzy—sometimes recklessly—used it to the fullest. For awhile he fought an 85 MPH duel with Chevalier René de Knyff on one of the big Panhards but left him nearly a quarter hour's worth of dust at the finish, covering the 327 miles in 6 hours and 39 minutes for a 49.2 MPH average. It had been a worthwhile endeavour. One source records that five million dollars in orders trace-able to Gordon Bennett publicity promptly flowed into Germany and helped pave the way for the next page in the Mercedes story.

*Chapter* 3

# The Great Grand Prix Cars

Mercedes fortunes have traditionally risen with its racing victories. Even today, much of Daimler-Benz's success in the salesrooms can be traced to the cachet of its spectacular postwar showing on the Grand Prix and sports car circuits and its later victories in stock car and rally competitions. The early 1900s found Daimler Motoren Gesellschaft totally dedicated to racing and the rewards— financial and technical—which it brought. And no race was more thoroughly prepared for than the 1904 Gordon Bennett.

After Jenatzy's victory at Ballyshannon, Germany, of course, became the host nation for the Gordon Bennett the following year, and took it upon herself to demonstrate to the world just how a great race should be organized and run. The spectacle at the Taunus circuit near Homburg that year was something to recall the opulence of Caesar's Circus Maximus combined with the pageantry of a jousting tournament out of Camelot. The Kaiser took a personal interest in the event and is said to have had a hand in designing the columned and garland-festooned stands and the formal boxes for the diplomatic corps. Twin bands across the track from each other contested to fill the air with *Preussens Gloria*. The week before the race was filled with official receptions and great balls. The grand and graceful style of an era drawing to a close was still the order of the day—polished marble floors, great Bohemian crystal chandeliers, banks of violins sliding out Strauss waltzes.

German thoroughness and an elite sense of organization were not to permit a repeat of the Paris-Madrid disaster. Five thousand troops were detached from the German army to see that no one set foot on the course while the cars were moving. No one did. It is to the great credit of the organizers that there was not a single casualty in the race, even among the drivers who could concentrate on driving without dodging pedestrians. A system of control points and a communication network completed a set of race preparations that rivaled those of modern times.

Camille Jenatzy and Germany's great hope for victory, the mighty Ninety Mercedes, prepared with no less diligence. Unlike a couple of drivers who showed up shortly before the race and asked for a road map, Jenatzy spent every permissible minute on the course memorizing the curves and straights and gauging shift points. After a while, his runs over the 318 mile course became so pat and predictable that farmers out in the countryside were telling time by arrival of the big white Mercedes. As an extra incentive, Clarence Dinsmore had bought the Ninety that Jenatzy would drive in the Gordon Bennett and promised its pilot $20,000 for a first place.

Competition was stiff on that warmish June morning of the 1904 Gordon Bennett; eighteen other cars including four other Nineties, three big 75 HP FIATs (one driven by Vicenzo Lancia), and a half dozen 100 HP cars of assorted

A Benz "Parsifal" sport phaeton of 1903/1904. Resulting from the stiff competition of Mercedes cars, Benz hired the French designer Marius Barbaroux to update his cars and the "Parsifal" was one of the results. It was not particularly successful, but marked the Benz transition from pioneer to modern concepts. (*Courtesy, Daimler-Benz*)

origin. But the big threat was Leon Théry on a quite sophisticated French-built Richard Brasier. Close attention had been paid to suspension and the Brasier was one of the first cars to be fitted with shock absorbers. Jenatzy drove true to his nickname, "The Red Devil", but the luck of the Ninety held. A fuel miscalculation at one point cost him precious minutes and at another the very fates seemed against him by sending a train across his path (at 90 MPH!) to further break his pace. Meanwhile, Théry was also holding true to his nickname, "The Chronometer", and setting up some very fast and regular times. Ultimately, he prevailed over Jenatzy by just over eleven minutes. It was a crushing blow to Mercedes and German pride, but it had been a grand and memorable race run in the best traditions of the sport and one which would serve as a model of efficiency for years to come.

"The Race To Death" was what the newspapers called the famous and fatal Paris to Madrid race of 1903. So many spectators and participants were killed that the race was ended even before it reached the French border. The car is a 1903 Benz driven by Barbarou. The pioneer sports car in this race reached speeds of 80 to 90 MPH over impossible roads often filled with fascinated spectators. (*Courtesy, Daimler-Benz*)

COUPE
GORDON BENNET

In 1899, James Gordon Bennett, the American newspaper publisher, decided to advance the cause of motoring by sponsoring a great annual international race and had this trophy, the *Coupe Internationale*, created for the victor. Mercedes won the trophy in the exciting 1903 Gordon Bennett at Ballyshannon, Ireland and France won it the next year when the Bennett was held in Germany. (*Courtesy, Automobile Club de France*)

A second place could hardly dampen the Daimler enthusiasm for racing, and the next reply was a 120 HP four cylinder car powered by a mammoth fourteen litre engine. Valuable improvements were made in engine design, but the day of the giant four cylinder cars was beginning to pass. The car did not account for itself particularly well in racing (it ate up tires nearly as fast as it did gasoline) and in 1906 attention was turned to a new six cylinder overhead valve racing car also of 120 HP. Likewise, this car did not add any great lustre to the Daimler record books, which may be explained by the fact that while other makers were beginning to rival DMG's eminence in the high performance field, the company was in a period of transition and beginning to reach for other concepts. A 70 HP touring version of the new six cylinder was, however, quite successful.

Basically, DMG was in a sound position; there was nothing on the scene to challenge Mercedes touring cars seriously and for private sportsmen the Ninety remained in production all the way to 1914. This was fortunate, for on April Fool's Day, 1907, the company lost the invaluable services of Wilhelm Maybach. The power beside the throne at Daimler's (and after 1900, behind it) had finally tired of captaining someone else's business and left to start one of his own. Setting up near the Zeppelin works on Lake Constance, he built engines for the great airships. The business grew and diversified and eventually got back to embrace automobiles, including a V-12 that appeared in 1930.

Maybach was succeeded as Chief Engineer by Gottlieb Daimler's son Paul. The selection was hardly nepotism for Paul Daimler was a talented engineer and for three years had charge of the Austro-Daimler works at Weiner-Neustadt. As his first project, young Daimler decided to have a try at the 1908 French Grand Prix, the rules for which now merely limited bore size to 155mm and minimum

Pristinely posed Mercedes Grand Prix car of 1908, the final expression of the 'great chain driven multi-litered cars which brought such glamour to the early days of racing. (*Courtesy*,

The 1908 Grand Prix Mercedes was Paul Daimler's first major project following Wilhelm Maybach's departure from DMG. The engine was designed with off-set connecting rods to shorten engine length. (*Courtesy, Daimler-Benz*)

Mercedes's arch rival in the 1908 French Grand Prix was this 150 HP Benz, designed by a brilliant young engineer named Hans Nibel who was to influence Benz and, later, Mercedes-Benz cars up to the present day. (Courtesy, Daimler-Benz)

weight to 1100 kilograms. The result was the last of its breed. The 1908 Grand Prix Mercedes was the final expression of the big chain-driven four-cylinder cars which had given such glamour to the Homeric age of racing just after the turn of the century. It was on cars like these that the great goggled giants like Jenatzy, Werner, and De Caters blasted through clouds of blinding dust to the crisp clashing of chains on sprockets in races that reached halfway across a continent.

The latest Grand Prix Mercedes represented a distillation of all Daimler experience in the pioneering era plus a few new twists which made it a quite novel machine. Its four cylinder 155 x 180 mm 12.8 litre engine, which could put out 135 HP at 1400 RPM, was a quite intriguing piece of work. To shorten the engine, Daimler had designed the connecting rods to run at an offset or oblique angle to the crankshaft. The overhead inlet valves were actuated by a camshaft on one side of the engine and the exhaust valves by another camshaft on the opposite side.

Mercedes was not without formidable competition in the 1908 French Grand Prix. There were forty-six entries and the most serious threat came in the form of the fearsome 1908 Benz Grand Prix car. As we have seen, Benz was struggling to break out of its archly conservative mould and the mildly successful Barbaroux had recently been replaced as Chief Engineer by Hans Nibel. Benz directors showed great acumen in recognizing the potential in this extraordinarily talented young engineer. Nibel was to become one of the great geniuses of automotive design and would vastly influence the course of Benz and, later, Mercedes-Benz cars all the way up to the present day. For 1908, Nibel developed a racing car from a Benz touring chassis, substituting chain drive for the now normal shaft drive. Although archaic for touring, chain drive still held advantages for

Christian Lautenschlager takes a curve on the Dieppe circuit in his 12.8 litre 1908 Mercedes Grand Prix car. Some of the 300,000 spectators line the route. (*Courtesy, Daimler-Benz*)

Pits, actually wood lined dug-outs (see left), were used for the first time in the 1908 French Grand Prix. It was a race of attrition on the primitive tires of 1908, as Lautenschlager's right front wheel indicates. Mercedes used Michelin demountable rims for the first time. (*Courtesy, Daimler-Benz*)

racing such as lower unsprung weight and a quick change of rear axle ratios by switching sprockets. Restricted by the rules to a 155 mm bore, Nibel used a daringly long 200 mm stroke in his 150 HP engine, which accounted for some frightening piston speeds. Christening came in the form of a resounding victory in a rugged race between St. Petersburg and Moscow over roads that would probably have looked familiar to Peter the Great.

The French Grand Prix of 1908 was run at Dieppe on a very carefully laid out circuit spread over forty-seven miles. The organizers coined a new word in the racing lexicon by providing "pits" for the service crews which were just that, dug-outs close by the stands. The race soon developed into a battle royal between the Mercedes under a talented young driver named Christian Lautenschlager and the big Benz driven by Victor Héméry. Both had enormous power in reserve which they were hesitant to use because in 1908 tire makers had a long way to go to catch up with automobile makers. One wrong move could easily cost a set of tires and some cars in the race had over a dozen tire changes. Great speed was possible, however, if you took your mind off the rubber for a few minutes; Otto Salzer on a Mercedes set the lap record at 78.6 MPH in 36½ minutes. Daimler did alleviate the disturbing tire problem a little by going over to Michelin demountable rims. Previously, worn tires had to be literally wrenched from the permanently attached wheels in a rather terrifying operation. Both Héméry and Lautenschlager called frequently at the pits for fresh rubber and there was much nail-biting in the Mercedes dug-out during Lautenschlager's last laps while he was racing on the last set of tires in sight. It was a nip and tuck, classic contest between the two German firms which now had grown into great rivals both on and off the track, but Lautenschlager took it for Mercedes with a 69 MPH average over the 477 miles of right angles and hills while 300,000 spectators cheered him on.

In the next few years DMG found Benz a determined adversary on the circuits and 1913 was a good example of how much a threat Benz had become. That year Mercedes recorded thirteen racing victories and Benz twenty-nine! And beyond that Benz profited handsomely from the publicity of Nibel's pet project, the gargantuan "Blitzen Benz" land speed record car. Working with the 1908 Grand Prix car as a base, Nibel bored out the engine to an astronomical 21.5 litres (1312 cubic inches), and the four huge cylinders (185 x 200 mm) put out about fifty horsepower each at 1600 RPM. Nibel used a special 112-inch wheelbase chassis to carry the monster engine with a forked front axle, chain

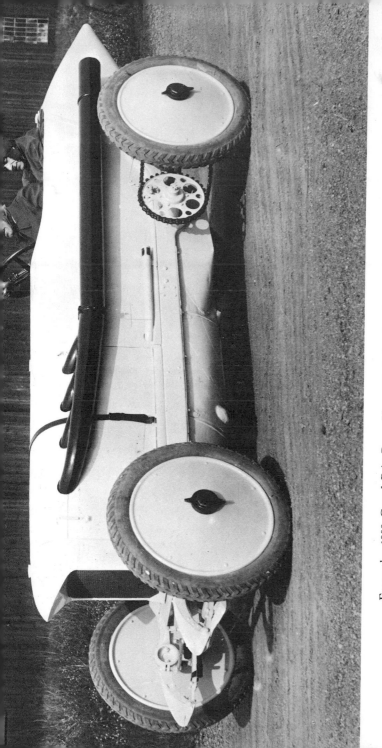

From the 1908 Grand Prix Benz, Hans Nibel developed a remarkable 21.5 litre land speed record car called the *Blitzen Benz* which the American driver Bob Burman drove at 141.7 MPH on Daytona Beach in 1911. The record stood for 15 years. (*Courtesy, Daimler-Benz*)

*Der Blitzen Benz,* complete with the imperial German eagle painted on the side, at Indianapolis Motor Speedway in 1912. Ralph De Palma is at the wheel. (*Courtesy, Indianapolis Motor Speedway*)

drive, and a frame drilled for lightness. The whole bizarre affair was then clothed in an aerodynamic body. At first outing the "Blitzen Benz" set a new world's record of 127.4 MPH at Brooklands Track in England, but later when the car came to America Bob Burman took it to its ultimate velocity of 141.7 MPH at Daytona Beach, a record which stood for fifteen years until 1924. Mercedes and Benz were both active in American racing at this time, Benz taking the first two places of the American Grand Prize in Savannah in 1910 and Ralph De Palma taking a Mercedes to victory in the 1912 Vanderbilt Cup at Milwaukee.

Despite its emoluments, Grand Prix racing was—and is—an enormously expensive affair. So, after the 1908 French Grand Prix the French, who were more than mildly displeased with the results, started a campaign to "kick the habit." They were moderately successful, and European Grand Prix racing fairly well languished until Gallic enthusiasm revived and it was decided to stage a Grand Prix in the grand manner for 1914. The chapter was finally closed on the age of the leviathans when the new formula for 1914 was announced; displacement could be no more than 4.5 litres or about one third of that of the typical racing car which was usually fielded. Clearly, the emphasis had now shifted to efficient engineering rather than sheer brutish engine size.

Paul Daimler now set to work to design a new Grand Prix car which would be wholly his own, for the 1908 car had been built largely in the image of Wilhelm Maybach. In the intervening years Mercedes had gained considerable experience with aircraft engines (some of which were installed in racing chassis!), and Daimler promptly put this knowledge to work in his 1914 car. What he came up with may well be regarded as his *piéce de resistance*, a car very nearly as revolutionary as the original Mercedes had been back in 1901.

For the first time an overhead camshaft was used, which actuated the four inclined valves per cylinder (two overhead inlet and two exhaust), and to ensure complete and immediate combustion, four spark plugs per cylinder were fitted. Following aircraft precedent, the water jackets around the individual cylinders were built separately of sheet steel and welded into place, a much more expensive but vastly superior method. An efficient pressure lubrication system was used, quite necessary in an engine that could sustain 3200 RPM for long periods, a unique feat for 1914.

The 1914 Grand Prix Mercedes looked the part of the worldbeater that it promised to be. The driver's line of

Ralph De Palma, one of the great names in American racing, was often mounted on a Mercedes. At right, he races to victory in the 1912 Vanderbilt Cup at Milwaukee. De Palma also won the 1915 Indianapolis "500" on a Mercedes. (*Courtesy, Indianapolis Motor Speedway*)

Ralph De Palma at the wheel of a special aero-engined 80 HP chain-drive Mercedes (based on the 1908 G.P. car) which was intended for the 1914 Indianapolis "500" but which did not run. (*Courtesy, Indianapolis Motor Speedway*)

The 4½ litre, overhead-cam engine of the 1914 G.P. car was derived from aircraft practice

The Mercedes team just before the 1914 French Grand Prix. Left to right: Pilette, Lautenschlager, Wagner, Sailer, and Salzer. (*Courtesy, Daimler-Benz*)

sight had been dropped about a foot below the 1908 racer and the 1914 car looked rakishly modern by comparison. Its visual image was greatly enhanced by the introduction of the Vee radiator which not only was aerodynamically sound but which lent an arrogant elegance to the Mercedes frontal facade which perseveres today. In 1908, the famous three-pointed star had been adopted as the Mercedes trademark and a star (as yet without the circle around it) graced each side of the radiator shell on the 1914 Grand Prix Mercedes.

So, Paul Daimler had a fast (112–115 MPH), high-revving, and very reliable racing car which incorporated more automotive experience and innovation under sheet steel than any other single car. This plus good drivers would have been enough for most makers, but it was not nearly enough for Mercedes. In April, some three months before the race, a very organized team of seven cars showed up on the challenging but beautifully conceived 23.3 mile circuit near Lyons. Practice went on with perfect Prussian precision. Fourteen hours daily the drivers toured the track, plotted shift and cut-off points, how fast curves could be taken, and then compared notes on it all under the direction of a newcomer on the racing scene, the team manager whose word was law. Then, back to Stuttgart where gear ratios and even wheelbase lengths were custom tailored to the Lyons circuit. Then back again to France for more practice with the altered cars.

It was clear that Mercedes was leaving as little as possible to chance, which was a smart idea considering the highly favored French competition. Peugeot had perfected some very sophisticated machinery (they won the Indianapolis "500" in 1913 and a host of European races) and their forte for 1914 was the first use of four-wheel brakes in Grand Prix racing. For the most part, the ability to go usually outstripped the ability to stop in early cars, and of course brakes at each corner gave the Peugeot a decided advantage in curves. In its extensive trials, Mercedes had tested four-wheel brakes but decided there was not enough time to perfect them, so all five Mercedes entries were to do battle using the usual rear-wheel brakes.

Peugeot's great strength and crowd pleaser was its star driver, Georges Boillot, who could handle a car the way some men handle a dueling pistol, and with enough showmanship to delight the French sense of flair. With the extruded Gallic lower lip, casual toss of the right hand, and a "Mais certainment!", fifty million Frenchmen were supremely confident that Georges Boillot could do no less than win. The Germans on the other hand were very close mouthed, and had reasoned that an adversary's greatest strength can also be his greatest weakness. It was in this race that the world would see the first great example of team strategy at work. For the first time in racing, a team would

Christian Lautenschlager at speed in number 28, the winning car of the 1914 French Grand Prix. (*Courtesy, Daimler-Benz*)

function as a *unit* under a pre-conceived plan and would be completely obedient to pit signals from the team manager and master tactician. At the heart of that strategy was the vanity of Georges Boillot, a man who could not stand to be passed.

Each of the five Mercedes drivers had an assigned task. The most important, and probably the most thankless, went to Max Sailer in Number 14 whose job it was to attack Boillot from the first lap. If necessary, Number 14 was to be regarded as expendable in pushing the Frenchman to the breaking point. Christian Lautenschlager in Number 28 was to move into the hole opened up for him by Sailer, and Otto Salzer and Louis Wagner in Numbers 39 and 40 were to lay back and wait for pit signals to follow Lautenschlager. Theodore Pilette was to be held in reserve against the unforeseen.

Boillot set up a scorching first lap time of 21 minutes and 29 seconds for the curvey 23.3 miles, from a standing start. The predominantly French crowds were re-assured as "le premier conducteur de France" screamed by the 2½ mile stretch in front of the new $50,000 stands. But their security was shaken a little when Max Sailer's time went up on the board across the track—18 seconds faster than the Peugeot despite the Mercedes' two-wheel brakes. There were two reasons for this. Although Boillot could hold his speed longer going into curves by virtue of his four-wheel brakes, Sailer could out-accelerate him like a rifle bullet on the straights. And secondly, Sailer's instructions were to throw everything he and the car had into the *beginning* of the race, luring Boillot to do the same. On the second lap, Sailer more than doubled his lead and the gap grew with each orbit. Meanwhile, Lautenschlager, Salzer, and Wagner hung back, comfortably "towing" or slip streaming behind other cars to conserve fuel. By the sixth lap, the strain accounted for Sailer's crankshaft and Boillot thankfully saw Mercedes Number 14 trickle off to the roadside.

Now, one could almost hear the mental computers clicking in the Mercedes pit. Signals went out for Christian Lautenschlager to move up to challenge Boillot, and for Otto Salzer and Louis Wagner to cautiously move in behind to support him and to cut off the leaders from the rest of the pack. The only significant obstacle now remaining besides Boillot himself was Jules Goux in the other Peugeot, and by mid-point he was safely astern of Salzer and Wagner. At about this time, Lautenschlager dropped out for refueling but amazingly regained his second place within a single lap, Salzer and Wagner "parting the Red Sea" to let him through to press the attack on Boillot.

By the sixteenth lap, Boillot was still gallantly holding his pursuers by about two minutes. Something was wrong. The Mercedes plan for blowing the Peugeot had called for its demise before now. But behind Boillot grew a low throated, high revving roar prophetically like a bi-plane peeling off into a dog fight. On the straights where the Mercedes revved up and accelerated only the sound of machine guns was missing. It was on this lap that the pit put out signals to administer the *coup de grace*. Mustachioed Christian Lautenschlager, who resembled film-actor Adolph Menjou, closed the gap to a scant fourteen seconds within the next lap and two laps later had established a full minute lead. Salzer and Wagner were poised seconds behind Boillot, ready to take him on the final round. But then a heart breaking thing happened. Just half a lap or about ten minutes from the finish the over-revved Peugeot gave up the ghost and trundled to a stop. (The announcement to the press was a snapped rear axle, but valve failure was the real *causa mortis*.) It was almost an anti-climax as Lautenschlager, Wagner, and Salzer swept by the finish for a triumvi-

The 1914 French Grand Prix saw the first use of organized team strategy under the direction of a team manager. Max Sailer in number 14 was assigned the task of wearing down Georges

A magnificent early racing picture; Christian Lautenschlager rounds a curve in the French Grand Prix at Lyons and heads for home as his riding mechanic checks rear tire wear. *(Courtesy, Daimler-Benz)*

Ralph De Palma acquired one of the victorious 1914 Mercedes racers and won the 1915 Indianapolis "500" with it. The "wasp tail" was an American addition. (*Courtesy, Indianapolis Motor Speedway*)

rate victory, greeted by thousands of dour French faces. Six days before, Archduke Franz Ferdinand had been shot in Sarajevo and exactly one month after the Mercedes victory Germany declared war on France. The 1914 French Grand Prix had held more than sporting significance.

There is an interesting epilogue to the story of the 1914 Grand Prix Mercedes. One of the Lyons cars was acquired by Ralph De Palma who brought it to America and won the 1915 Indianapolis "500" with it. Another one, according to one story, was pounced upon by some primeval James Bond of the British secret service who boxed it up and sent it to London for study. Actually, the car was quite conventionally sent to the English Mercedes concessionaires who exhibited it to a curious British public. When the war came, the car was turned over to Rolls-Royce who studied its aero engine aspects to their profit. Much the same thing, although rather more blatantly, was done by the Americans with Ralph De Palma's car. It was hardly a secret that the famous World War I "Liberty" engine was actually a watered down version of the Mercedes using only two valves per cylinder instead of the original four.

Despite an intervening war and much new technology, the 1914 Grand Prix Mercedes was well ahead of its time and did not die easily. A dozen years later when Ferdinand Porsche was chief engineer at Mercedes he still found enough interest in the old car to fit it with a supercharger and send it to the Semmering Hill Climb where it proceeded to beat the pants off everything in sight, including Porsche's newest six cylinder, six liter supercharged monsters! And, believe it or not, in 1933 when the words "Grand Prix" again came often to the lips, Mercedes-Benz engineers went back to 1914 to study the welded up construction of the grand old engine and promptly adapted it to their newest Grand Prix car.

# Chapter 4

# The Screaming Mercedes

Shortly before he left the Daimler enterprise, Wilhelm Maybach began to experiment with six-cylinder automobiles. By 1906 he had a high powered six-cylinder racing car and a six-cylinder tourer, although the 80 HP touring car of the following year was by far the most successful of the lot.

Paul Daimler picked up the concept of the smooth running, spirited six-cylinder car and just before World War I developed it into a very interesting, and ultimately very influential, car called the 28/95 (taxable horsepower/brake horsepower). He conceived of the car as what the Germans call a *Hoechsleistung-Tourenwagen*, a high performance touring car, or simply a comfortable car which could move well. To distill sufficient spirit, he turned to DMG's recent aero engine experience and the new research which had gone into the 1914 Grand Prix cars. What he came up with, a 7.2 litre six-cylinder overhead-camshaft car, was an accurate harbinger of what was to come in the future in both philosophy and appearance.

Despite the spectacular success of the 1914 Grand Prix cars, Daimler was still feeling his way in adapting aero engine principles to automobiles. Airplane engines and the prolonged high speed for which the Grand Prix car was designed had much in common, but the 28/95 tourer was a different animal and required more flexibility for varying speeds. Accordingly, the earlier versions could be contrary and temperamental. However, almost anything could be forgiven just by looking at one of these cars. A sense of gloriously arrogant elegance exuded from the sharply Vee shaped radiator which cut deeply into the bonnet, and from the engine compartment curled three great nickel plated external exhaust pipes to give a very virile image of brute power. The exhausts were not, as legend has it, the trademark of a supercharged Mercedes. Although they were used extensively in the supercharger era, they actually preceded it considerably, appearing as early as the 1908 Grand Prix car. The big, solid, four-door open "Tourenwagens" were sparkling, effervescent machines, but the short wheelbase "Sportwagens" which appeared after the war were pure exhilaration to the mind's eye. And they were capable cars on road and track, too, accounting for themselves well in competition even years after they were technically obsolete.

The 28/95 had just gotten into production at the outbreak of World War I, and a plainly finished austerity model was continued almost immediately after the end of the war, which if nothing else was a masterpiece of corporate organization in the midst of economic chaos. The chassis price was about $7500. It was with one of these 28/95s that Mercedes scored its first success in its re-entry into post-war competition. And an imposing victory it was, too; won against the most unlikely odds.

In 1921 it was decided to enter a 28/95 in the Coppa

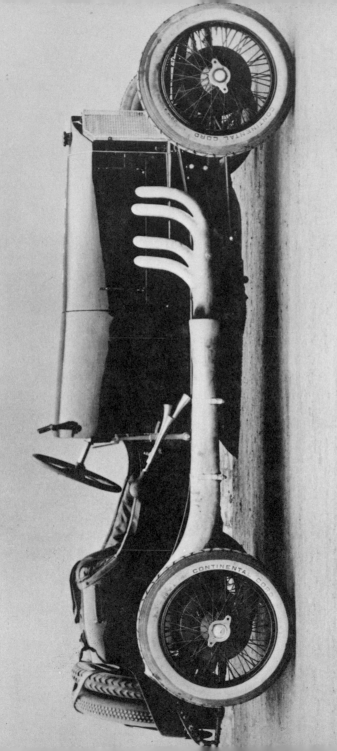

A prime example of Mercedes's small displacement supercharged *Hoechsleistungs-Rennwagen* —high efficiency racing car. This two-litre, 120 HP, four-cylinder car with Christian Werner up won both the Targa Florio and Coppa Floria, plus the Coppa Termini team prize in 1924. (*Courtesy, Daimler-Benz*)

Paul Daimler's big 28/95 high performance cars of 1914 had a sparkling, effervescent personality. This short wheelbase postwar sports version was the pride of its kind, and the car which started the succession of "the great white Mercedes" of the 1920s. (*Courtesy, Daimler-Benz*)

Florio, a particularly brutal race through the Sicilian mountains. Max Sailer, the pressure man of the 1914 French Grand Prix, was assigned to drive the Coppa 28/95 from Stuttgart to the starting line, which in those days was an endurance feat worthy of a gold medal in itself. The seriousness of the project was such that Sailer gathered all his relatives around him before he left and had a family portrait made. With calculable German preciseness, Sailer arrived in Sicily on schedule, proceeded to win the Coppa Florio (sports car class) and take second place in the Targa Florio (racing cars), and then promptly drove his Mercedes home. Daimler interest in the Coppa and Targa Florio events extended over the next few years and resulted in considerable success.

The First World War had taught Daimler Motoren

After some experience with smaller cars, Paul Daimler supercharged his 28/95 in 1922, and the big 7.2 litre car returned racing successes years after it was technically obsolete. (*Courtesy, Daimler-Benz*)

In 1921, Max Sailer drove a 28/95 Mercedes from the factory to Sicily, won the Coppa Florio, took second place in the Targa Florio, and then drove the big car back home—an epic feat of endurance and skill.

Gesellschaft many technical lessons, not the least of which was supercharging. Aero engine starvation at altitudes above 10,000 feet encouraged Daimler engineers to experiment with supercharging, literally force-feeding the engine with extra blasts of air and fuel. Gottlieb Daimler had toyed with the technique back in the 1880s, the American Chadwick car had used it with some success in 1908, and Marc Birkigt had tried using two extra cylinders as air pumps on an experimental version of the Alphonso XIII Hispano-Suiza. Daimler supercharged aero engines were operational by 1915 and Benz followed suit the next year. It was the combination of Daimler and Benz expertise which helped give German World War I planes technical, although not numerical, superiority over the Allied air fleets. Daimler's began building complete airplanes at Sindelfingen in 1915, and before the end of the war had 500 HP and 600 HP air engines in limited production.

The 28/95 was the likely candidate for postwar experiments with supercharging, and some writers have indicated it to have been the car used. Actually, Mercedes's first experience with a supercharged automobile was with another, much smaller car. In 1909, Daimler started building a curious sleeve valve engine under license from the American inventor Charles Y. Knight. The "Mercedes-Knight" was a complicated affair and quite expensive to produce, but it offered smooth silence and a ten percent power boost over a conventional engine of the same size. It was a happy marriage, and for a time even bore sweet fruit in competition, including victory in the Czar Nicholas Tour of 1910. Four models were built, the 10/30, 16/40, 16/45, and 16/50, and it was the 10/30 that was first fitted with a supercharger in 1919.

Daimler chose a Rootes type-two blower as the most suitable supercharging system for the 10/30. Running at three to four times engine speed and mounted forward in order to blow *through* the carburetor rather than to suck the air/gas mixture from it in the conventional way, the Mercedes supercharger produced a hair-raising scream when engaged. Over the next twenty years the Valkyrie cry of the big blower would herald the approach of an assortment of great

A two-litre supercharged Mercedes at Indianapolis in 1923. Max Sailer was to have driven the car, but was replaced by his brother Karl following a practice accident. The car finished eighth. (*Courtesy, Indianapolis Motor Speedway*)

DRIVER. CHRISTIAN WOERNER.

CAR MERCEDES. 500 MILE RACE 1923.

INDIANAPOLIS MOTOR SPEEDWAY.

Christian Werner at Indianapolis in 1923 in his two-litre supercharged 120 HP four-cylinder

Mercedes and Mercedes-Benz cars, and would become almost as famous a trademark as the silver star itself.

The early tests had been very encouraging and Daimler was convinced that the supercharger was the wave of the future. So he pressed the accelerator hard on his supercharged Mercedes cars, both literally and figuratively. In 1921, he exhibited a pair of poppet-valved, supercharged cars at the Berlin Motor Show; the 1.5 litre four-cylinder "6/25/40" (taxable Hp/brake HP/HP with supercharger engaged) and the 2.6 litre "10/40/65", also four cylinders. The smaller car formed part of a carefully devised plan to sweep the 1922 Coppa and Targa Florio. The attack was three-pronged, consisting of a trio of 1914 Grand Prix cars (unsupercharged) at the top, a pair of newly supercharged 28/95s, and two little 1.5 litre 6/25/40s in racing trim. Count Guilio Masetti, a very accomplished Italian driver, won the rough and tumble Targa Florio in a 1914 Grand Prix car with the other G.P. cars just behind him in number two and four spots. The other Mercedes entries all did well in their respective categories to sprinkle a splendid shower of three pointed stars over the scene.

The small supercharged cars had not quite been the hit of the show, but nevertheless the concept of the highly efficient supercharged "mini-racer" was developed further and resulted in a quite successful two-litre, four-cylinder, supercharged car developing 120 HP. It was with one of these cars that Christian Werner scored his famous *Doppleseig*—double victory—by winning both the Coppa Florio and Targa Florio in 1924. Within their class, it was another 1-2-3 win for Mercedes with Lautenschlager in the second car and in the third a man whose name was to become synonymous with Mercedes and racing—Alfred Neubauer.

A pair of the two litres had been less successful the year before at the Indianapolis "500". Christian Werner took only eleventh place in his number sixteen and Karl Sailer, driving for his brother Max who had been injured during practice, made eighth place in number fifteen. However, as an overall concept the small displacement supercharged car had clearly come into its own. In a single year (1924), Daimler and Benz cars recorded 269 racing successes and ninety-three of them are credited to Mercedes 1.5 and two-litre supercharged cars. The next link in the chain of development of the small *Hoechsliestung-Rennwagen* led to another two-litre car with dual overhead camshafts, eight cylinders, and 160 HP. This jewel-like, high efficiency little machine was one of mixed blessings and, as we shall see in the next chapter, was perhaps the most enigmatic of all Mercedes cars.

# Chapter 5

# *Dr. Porsche Comes to Stuttgart*

Gene Fowler, the author, once suggested that money "is something to be thrown off the back ends of trains," and did his level best to live up to that philosophy. A rather more satisfying, but nearly as costly, thing to do with surplus cash in the days of his literary exploits was to invest in one of Herr Doktor Ferdinand Porsche's "great white Mercedes" cars which flourished concurrently with Mr. Fowler's effulgent philosophy.

Ferdinand Porsche furnished *Daimler Motoren Gesellschaft*—which became *Daimler-Benz Aktiengesellschaft* during his reign there—with the stuff of which dreams, legends, and the pleasanter hallucinations are spun. Put more pedestrianly, he built the most inspiringly awesome road machines ever to put rubber to concrete. Porsche was an indisputably brilliant man of occasionally unorthodox leanings. He would like as not show up in the drawing office in a loden green shooting suit. But while the starched shirt German formalists in the front office might think of him as an eccentric Austrian hillbilly, they could not lightly

Pensive portrait of Dr. Ferdinand Porsche, creator of the epic "S" series Mercedes-Benz cars, plus scores of other designs, during his five-year stay at Stuttgart. Porsche ranks among the most prolific and influential automotive designers in history. (*Courtesy, Daimler-Benz*)

dismiss the sixty-five outstanding designs which he produced during his five-year stay at Stuttgart.

Making things with metal came early into Ferdinand Porsche's life. The son of a Bohemian tinsmith, he was born the 3rd of September, 1875, which made him eleven years old when Karl Benz ran his first car. Shortly afterward, he was apprenticed to his father, and it was not long before his

interests sprawled well beyond the little shop in Maffers-
dorf. The new power sources, electricity and internal combustion, shared nearly equal places in his vivid and expanding imagination. After getting a hard-won basic technical
education—he had less formal technological training than
either Daimler or Benz—he came to work for the imperial
coachbuilder to Emperor Franz Josef in Vienna. Disdaining
the noise, smell, and vibration of the internal combustion
engine, the Emperor specified that his first motorcar should
be an electric. The coachbuilder, Lohner, struggled with
the problem and then turned to Porsche. The young engineer, not yet twenty-five years old, responded with an electric car which so pleased Franz Josef that he sent it out to
international exhibitions to show what Austria could do.

Despite everyone's satisfaction with the Porsche-Lohner
electric (which survives today in a Vienna museum) and
Camille Jenatzy's 1899 speed record of 65 MPH in a Jeantaud electric car, Porsche realized that the future of an
automobile dependent upon inefficient batteries held little
promise. So, he switched his allegiance to gas engines. His
abilities at this stage can be gauged by the fact that he was
able to walk into Daimler's Austrian factory at Weiner-
Neustadt and take over Paul Daimler's job as Chief Engineer in 1906. Daimler of course was returning to the main
plant at Stuttgart to succeed his late father's late friend and
collaborator Wilhelm Maybach.

Porsche's first assignment at Austro-Daimler had illustrious precedent. The story of how Emil Jellinek came to
Daimler's in 1900 and agreed to underwrite the production
of the new high performance car which he urged into existence if it would be named for his daughter Mercedes has
now passed into legend. But what is not so well known was
that Jellinek still had another daughter on his hands with no
automobile named after her. To render justice and ensure

"You looked, you ran your hand over the pristinely white lacquered fenders, you sat on the lush red leather, you drove. Then you either bought it or inwardly wept." (*Courtesy,*

domestic tranquility, Jellinek induced *Osterreichische-Daimler* to name its new Porsche-designed car the "Maja".

This car appeared during Porsche's first year at Austro-Daimler and underwent considerable development over the next few years. It was not, however, ready to compete in the interesting "Kaiserpreis" race held in Germany in 1907. The Kaiser had decreed that the maximum displacement would be eight litres which, in those days of monster slow-revving engines, excluded the all-out racers. Working with a standard Mercedes chassis which was produced at Weiner-Neustadt, Porsche altered it to suit himself and fitted it with an electric transmission of his own design. The Kaiserpreis attracted about eighty entries and unfortunately Porsche's car —entered as the "Mercedes Mixte"—did not qualify in the pre-race trials.

On a Mercedes "K" chassis, the Parisian coachbuilder, Saoutchik, built this magnificent machine for a French diplomat. The car could be used three ways; as a formal Sedan de Ville (as shown), a closed car, or a sporty open phaeton with fold-up rear windscreen. (Owner: Bud Cohn)

In 1910, Prince Henry of Prussia, brother to the Kaiser and ardent automobile afficionado, sponsored "The Prince Henry of Prussia Reliability Trials". This event eventually gravitated toward a combination grand tour and sports car rally and became a "fun thing" laced with liberal stops at the great houses of wealthy sportsmen along the way where cars and drivers both could refuel.

The Trials received a lot of publicity and many auto makers went to building special cars to compete. Porsche had been developing the "Maja" and now unveiled a special "Prince Henry" version, just as Vauxhall did in England. This time the gearbox was standard, not electric, and the chassis was not revolutionary. But the machine's forte lay in its brilliantly designed 5.7-litre, four-cylinder, overhead-camshaft, inclined-valve engine which could develop 90 to 100 horsepower with extreme efficiency and deliver nearly 90 MPH. In 1910, Porsche's "Prince Henry" represented a brave and brilliant step toward the small-displacement, high-efficiency engine of the future. It is interesting to compare it with the "Sixty" Mercedes which had been the paragon of road machines just a few years before. The "Sixty" required 9.2 litres to produce its peak sixty horse-power, while the Austro-Daimler could put out nearly forty percent more power with not much more than half the displacement. Three cars were entered in the Trials— Porsche himself drove one—and they surpassed all expectations by sweeping home in a neat 1-2-3 victory.

Over the next few years, Porsche proved himself to be a creative engineer ranking with Marc Birkigt, Sir Henry Royce, and Walter Owen Bentley. For sheer diversity of ideas he was in the stratospheric class of the great Ettore Bugatti himself. But it became progressively clearer that Porsche was out of his element in the provincialism of Austro-Daimler. So, in the spring of 1923 Dr. Porsche came

Porsche's 6.8 litre "S" type Mercedes-Benz got its initiation into racing at the 1927 German Grand Prix, which opened the great Nurburgring circuit. The "S" cars, which were sports cars which could run successfully in full Grand Prix events, faithfully delivered the Mercedes trademark 1-2-3 win. (*Courtesy, Daimler-Benz*)

to Stuttgart to replace Paul Daimler as Chief Engineer (for the second time) and to begin the most fabulous phase of his career.

When Ferdinand Porsche took up his duties at *Daimler Motoren Gesellschaft,* high among its concerns were the big 7.2 litre 28/95 sports tourer developed since 1914 by Paul Daimler, and a series of small displacement high efficiency supercharged racing cars. The last of these, a supercharged, two-litre, double overhead-camshaft straight eight, was giving problems and it was handed over to Porsche to iron out the bugs. The two-litre was powerful—160 HP and up to 8000 RPM—and violently fast, but it lacked the revered

German virtue of predictability. One trip might be a textbook run and the next might yield fouled plugs and spotty performance.

The firm Porsche hand made a solid imprint on the contrary little car; after he had shown it who was master it ran obediently and well. It was, however, destined to have a cloud over its countenance. One of the revised two-litres was entered for the Italian Grand Prix at Monza in 1924 to be driven by Count Louis Zborowski. The son of one of the most colorful characters of early racing, Count Eliot Zborowski, he cherished his parent's early love for Mercedes and fathered the famous series of four Mercedes-based "Chitty-Bang-Bang" cars. It will be recalled that Zborowski senior was killed driving a "Sixty" Mercedes in the 1903 Nice Speed Week races. Sadly, his son now suffered the same fate, also driving a Mercedes, in the Italian Grand Prix when his two-litre skidded on an oil slick. The most profound irony of all was that Count Louis was wearing those very same cuff links that his father had worn that day at Nice twenty-one years earlier.

Naturally, many stories circulated about the Zborowski crash and one of them was that the two-litre was unsafe. This was given some credibility by the fact that the remaining cars were withdrawn from the race—actually out of respect—and did not appear again in competition for many months. However, while it is true that the two-litre chassis design was perhaps not up to the highly developed engine, the car was a good one and proved it by winning twenty-one out of the twenty-seven races in which it ran. Perfection of the two-litre was a good start, but a relatively minor notch on the Porsche coup stick.

Porsche now turned his mind to Paul Daimler's concept of the *Hoechsleistung-Tourenwagen* or high performance touring car as embodied in the 28/95. He had in mind a comfortable car of high spirits. What Walter Owen Bentley called "a car with long legs"; a car imbued with what the Germans would call *ausdauer*, the stamina to endure endless hours of flat-out driving. Porsche prudently kept the self-assured arrogant elegance of Daimler's car, especially the sharply Vee-shaped radiator and the Teutonic sense of solidity. But he had rather different ideas about what should go under the hood. For the first time in a Mercedes the crankcase and cylinders were formed in a one-piece aluminum casting. The overhead camshaft was, of course, retained, mounted on the cylinder head, and driven by silent helical gears. The whole was capped by a polished aluminum alloy cam cover and offered a very neat and orderly underhood picture. The supercharger had now become a standard fixture.

Porsche had responded to the project with the swiftness common to selfsure geniuses and created a pair of six cylinder cars which were the first born of a royal dynasty, the 15/70/100 and the 24/100/140. These were virtually two editions of the same car, the smaller a four-litre of 11.8 foot wheelbase and the larger a six-litre with a 12.3 foot wheelbase. These cars became the new prestige models for 1924, appearing usually as wood framed open touring cars with aluminum coachwork. In "The Annals of Mercedes-Benz Vehicles and Engines" published by Daimler-Benz in 1956 the cars are described as "the Stradivarius of the road", which is a description not to be tampered with.

Mercedes was now in another of its periodic withdrawals from Grand Prix racing and major effort could be expended on touring and sports cars. In 1926, Porsche released an improved version of the six-litre car. His re-thinking included shortening the wheelbase to 11.2 feet, for which the car was called the "K" type—"K" for *kurz* or short. In British horsepower nomenclature, the new car was the

33/180, which it is sometimes called in America, although "K" type seems simpler. Porsche now began his "displacement escalation" of the series by upping the engine to 6¼ litres which now put 160 HP under foot with the supercharger blowing.

The "K" type Mercedes properly began an era of legendary, Wagnerian flavored machines which was, for a few brief years, an automotive Camelot. Despite its great shortcoming, poor brakes, the "K" was a resplendent piece of machinery and quickly became an international status symbol for the affluent gentleman who was pleased to learn that he didn't really have quite everything until he had a supercharged Mercedes. The "K" cars were well received despite a stiff bare chassis price of $7500–$8000, plus $4000 or more for custom coachwork. In flights of fancy, rather more could be spent. Al Jolson, "The Jazz Singer", began with a "K" chassis and wound up with a $28,000 town car with gold fittings and bird-of-paradise design tapestry upholstery.

Another apparently unique "K" type Mercedes, now in the collection of Mr. M. L. "Bud" Cohn of Los Angeles, was created by the Parisian coachbuilder Saoutchik for a French diplomat. Mr. Cohn describes the interesting coachwork: "The car has a famous three position body; with the entire top up it is formal; with half the top up it is semiformal; with the top folded back, which recedes onto a rack and pinion on the rear end of the tonneau, it becomes a perfect and sporty touring car, and the beautiful wood which snaps over the edges gives it a luxurious look second to none." While the Cohn car may well be one of a kind, most "K"'s got premium treatment by coachbuilders.

That such cars as the "K" type Mercedes were created at all is more than mildly astounding, for the middle twenties were tenuous times in Germany. Inflation rose to such an economist's nightmare that it was possible to walk into a butcher shop with a market basket full of money and walk out with it half full of food. At the time, there were eighty-six motorcar makers in Germany and the competition was cut-throat. In the middle of it all *Daimler Motoren Gesellschaft* and *Benz und Cie* found cooperation more attractive than competition. The two companies had been informally associated since 1923 and formalized their relationship into amalgamation on the 28th/29th of June, 1926, to form a new company called *Daimler-Benz Aktiengesellschaft*. The Mercedes three pointed star and Benz laurel wreath were also amalgamated to form the present Mercedes-Benz insignia, which is certainly one of the most attractive logos in motordom.

The next year the Porsche push for the ultimate road machine of the day dropped into high gear when he inaugurated the epic "S" type (sports) Mercedes-Benz. By arching the frame sharply over the rear axle (less in front) and using underslung rear springs, Porsche slashed the height of the car to achieve a racy new low silhouette. Literage was boosted to 6.8 and a new supercharger producing eight pounds per square inch pressure was fitted, which now blew through two Pallas carburetors. The result was a heavy, hearty, muscular throb of high torque and low revs coupled to a dazzling sense of surfeit power. The car now had the easy flexibility which the old 28/95 had lacked; the big engine offered 3 to 103 MPH in top gear and delivered it with the unfaltering thrust of a locomotive. With proper tuning, more speed was possible. In 1928 an "S" type set the German sports car speed record with 110.4 MPH.

Porsche's big 6.8 litre engine was a masterwork of pure brute strength. Superficially, there seemed to be little claim to Bugatti-like finesse, yet the quality was so fantastically exacting and tolerances so close that the head gasket was the

Oil stained but victorious Otto Merz after the 1927 German Grand Prix in an "S" type with a racing stripe across the hood. The low silhouette which Porsche achieved by the arched

only gasket in the entire engine! If there was ever a classic example of engineering being perfectly matched to appearance the "S" series Mercedes-Benz cars of the Twenties was it. No matter how svelte or lush the coachwork that was fitted the car never lacked its charismatic character of menacing efficiency. The "S" cars faithfully followed Frank Lloyd Wright's precepts of "organic architecture" in which "form follows function" and, appropriately, Wright was a Mercedes fancier until he died. The lengthened hood and lowness of the "S" chassis was virgin material for the great custom coachbuilders to work with, and what many connoisseurs regard as the most beautiful automobiles ever created were built on this frame.

The visual vivacity of the Mercedes-Benz "S" type was enormous. The most frequently fitted body was an open sports tourer, sometimes equipped with the vestige of a rear seat reached by a natty little cut-away door just behind the doorless front compartment. Some bodies were more conservative than this *Sportmodell*, but whether they were sedate, dramatic, or bizzare (and there were some of each) they were *never* dull. Enough of the magic has come down through the years unchanged to make a great commercial success of Brooks Stevens's "Excalibur SS" replicas made from modern American components. Even though the Excalibur is not a Mercedes-Benz it is perhaps the nicest compliment Daimler-Benz has ever been given.

With the master Rudolf Caracciola often at the wheel, the "S" cars promptly went out and gathered honors by the bushel basket. In 1927, they opened the great new *Nurburgring* circuit—a sort of German WPA project brooded over by the picturesque Nurburg Castle—with a "Mercedes trademark" 1-2-3 victory. For the 1928 season alone, they took 53 victories and set 17 records. But no one seemed to care so much about that. You looked, you ran your hand

Rudolph Caracciola, the hero of Ards and the man considered to be the greatest driver of all time. Alfred Neubauer maintained that he never really "learned" to drive, but that he just "felt it" and the talent came to him instinctively. Neubauer characterized Caracciola's style as "soft and elegant, but very fast." (*Courtesy, Daimler-Benz*)

over the pristinely white lacquered fenders, you sat on the lush red leather, you drove. Then you either bought it or inwardly wept. With a $9700 bare chassis price and a total production of 146 cars there must have been a lot of suppressed tears.

On the "S" type, Porsche attacked in earnest a problem which plagued the whole series of "K" and "S" cars as long as he was at Stuttgart. In spite of the hair raising performance, braking was terrifying by modern standards and casual by contemporary measure. Although, one 1928 driver disputed this often-cited criticism by writing: "When you desire to stop the brakes smoothly but rapidly (!) reduce the speed as if a giant hand had clutched the car to arrest its progress." Porsche attacked the one bugaboo of his cars by fitting power assisted brakes with outrageously huge drums. This was a considerable improvement (the

Rudolf Caracciola sweeping along in Mercedes-Benz "SS" number 70 at the Ards Tourist Trophy in August, 1929. Heavy rain daunted other drivers but Caracciola's "visual radar" let him see his way through the cloudbursts to victory. (*Courtesy, Daimler-Benz*)

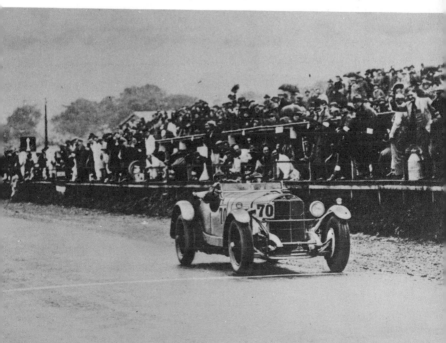

"K" required 145 feet to come to rest from 40 MPH!), although few drivers have ever claimed the "S" 's reluctance to halt as one of its endearing points.

Porsche's game of one-upsmanship moved inexorably on and the next echelon came in 1928 with the "SS" Mercedes-Benz. This car was known in England as the 38/250 and has occasionally been mistakenly referred to as *Sehr Schnell* (very fast). Actually, as confirmed by Daimler-Benz's competent public relations director, Artur Keser, the correct nomenclature is "Super Sport". But whatever you choose to call it, the revised Mercedes-Benz was Ferdinand Porsche done on a C.B. DeMille scale. Just as the name implied, everything was a "super" version of the "S" type. The engine was again enlarged, to 7.1 litres, and was fitted with an even more energetic supercharger to feed the mixture at ten pounds pressure. Horsepower rose to 225 with the blower going, and the price was "super", too, $10,800 to $12,100 for the chassis. The "SS" now superseded the "S" and remained in production until 1933 by which time 111 cars had been built.

A specially shortened version of the "SS", the rare and fully fabulous "SSK" ("K" for *kurz*, short), was brought out at about the same time. This esoteric machine was a plethora of plenty for the all-out sportsman who could look unblinkingly upon the $13,550 price tag on the unclothed chassis. The mechanics remained basically the same as for the "SS" (although a few hardy souls fitted their cars with the giant twelve pound "Elephant" blower), but the chassis was chopped from a 134 inch wheelbase to 116 inches. The effect of this strategy, besides lightening the car for greater speed, was to place the driver and his solitary passenger almost directly over the rear wheels (!) with nearly six feet of louvered hood stretched out before them. The aura of unbridled power was enormous even at rest and the sense of

The irrepressible elegance of the SSK Mercedes-Benz of 1928. This beauty, out after a light snow, was built by the custom coachbuilder, Papler, and carries the owner's coat of arms just below the door moulding. (*Courtesy, Daimler-Benz*)

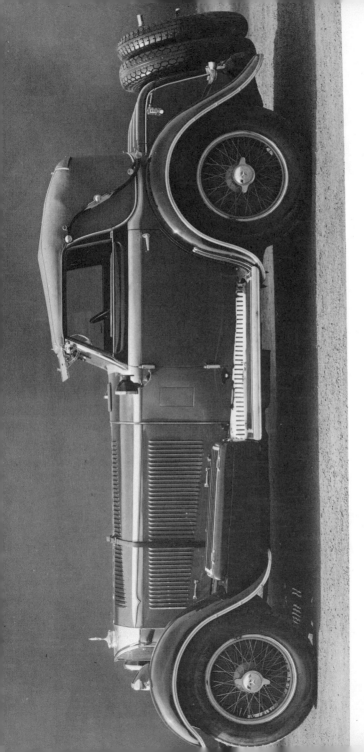

A car with charisma, the cherished SSK Mercedes-Benz. Built on an SS chassis specially shortened to 116-inch wheelbase, the SSK cost $13,550 plus coachwork. Thirty-three were built and eleven are still known to survive. (*Courtesy, Daimler-Benz*)

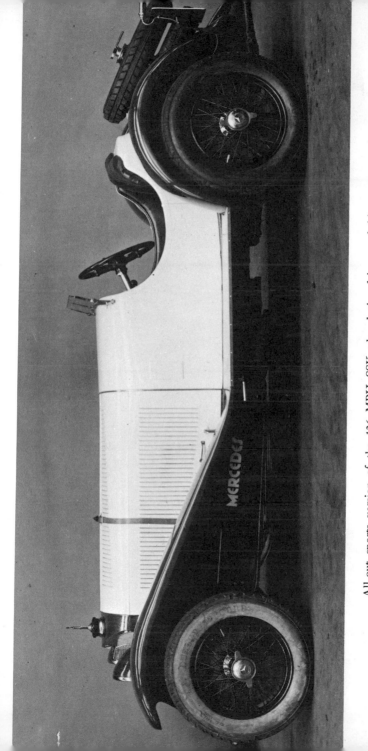

All-out sports version of the 126 MPH SSK placed the driver and his passenger almost directly over the rear wheels with nearly six feet of lowered white hood stretched out before them. (*Courtesy, Daimler-Benz*)

The Super Sport Kurz (short) done as a two-toned, open roadster with narrow little flip-down racing windscreens and stone guard over the radiator. (*Courtesy, Daimler-Benz*)

acceleration to a top speed of 126 MPH was prodigious. Some extraordinarily handsome roadster bodies were built on the SSK chassis, very possibly the most desirable cars of the entire "S" series that were offered for public sale. Certainly they were the scarcest. Only 33 SSKs were built from 1928 to 1932 and of this handful only one in every three is known to survive today, making them one of the rarest—and most expensive—classics.

The great "S" cars were excellent public relations pieces. Few people could afford them but everyone knew them, and by association they lent high lustre to the range of Mercedes-Benz bread and butter cars. A trio of such medium range automobiles called the "Stuttgart", "Mannheim", and "Nurburg" appeared shortly after the Daimler-Benz amalgamation in 1926. Some further attention was paid to the "Mannheim", which began life as a prosaic 3.1 litre tourer, and by 1929 had emerged from its cocoon as a mildly dazzling—and possibly the least known—Mercedes-Benz sports car. Mechanically, the 370S was an oddball. It combined a rather pedestrian L-head engine with such curiosa as a two-speed, vacuum-operated rear, a six-speed gearbox, and a straight-through exhaust system. Visually, the 370S was a subtly elegant machine endowed with scaled down lines lifted from the later "S" cars, but tempered with a flat Benz-type radiator. Although development of the 370S was carried on during Porsche's stay at Stuttgart, it was the pet project of Hans Nibel the Benz Chief Engineer who shared equal status with Porsche after the merger.

Anything larger than life and as legendary as Porsche's big six-cylinder Mercedes cars of the 1920s is bound to engender controversy. In the minds of many, these cars represent the automobile at its zenith. To others they were brutish and unsubtle. But they were real, and when the checkered flag dropped they seldom tarnished the legend.

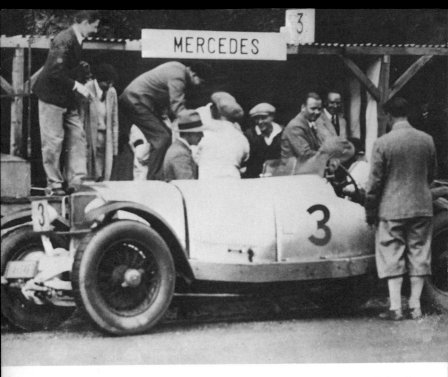

Number three SSK at the pits in the 1930 Irish Grand Prix. Caracciola required three hours and twenty-eight minutes to win the 300 mile race. (*Courtesy, Daimler-Benz*)

The "Mercedes steamroller" swept the great races of the Twenties and caught the popular fancy. Mercedes-Benz victories of the day read like a tour of the important racing circuits, and even to list them would be tedious. One triumph of man and machine, however, stands head and shoulders among the rest and cannot be denied—the great ride of Rudolf Caracciola at Ards.

Four Mercedes-Benz cars were entered for the Irish Tourist Trophy race in 1929. Caracciola and veteran Otto Merz drove the works-entered "SS" cars and there were two privately entered "S" types. All would do battle against a field of 61 cars which read like a royal roll call of the cream of the world's sports machinery and drivers. It prom-

Caracciola's SSK at the Irish Grand Prix in 1930. Caracciola finished first, Lord Howe fourth, and Sir Malcolm Campbell, sixth. (*Courtesy, Daimler-Benz*)

Three SSKs were entered in the 1930 Grand Prix of Ireland, driven by Rudolf Caracciola, Lord Howe, and Sir Malcolm Campbell. Here, Caracciola takes a sandbagged curve with Lord Howe close behind. (*Courtesy, Daimler-Benz*)

ised to be a fast and exciting race. Within a lap after the scrambling "Le Mans start" Caracciola was in the lead and handling the big white number 70 Mercedes-Benz like a violin in the hands of a virtuoso; braking at the instinctively correct instant before a curve, cornering the big car with the facility of a grocery cart changing aisles in a supermarket, biting the wheels into the dust once he was around, and then digging in the supercharged spurs with a supernatural scream to build up velocity for the straight up ahead. It was rare artistry as only Caracciola could do it. Not the mere mastery of man over metal, but a complete merger of man and machine.

Then, rain started to fall on the Ards circuit, became a downpour, and finally a deluge. Lap times increased, some cars pulled out entirely, and the other "SS" smashed a fender on a slippery curve. But as the others slowed down

A 6.8 litre "S" Mercedes-Benz of 1927 with rakish sports-tourer coachwork. The car was famous for its "demand" supercharger with its Valkyrie wail which cut in when the accelerator was pushed to the floor. (*Courtesy, Daimler-Benz*)

Caracciola gunned his supercharged 7.1 litres and streaked on through the sheets of water and the sea of mud. Years later in discussing the "soft and elegant but very fast" Caracciola style, Alfred Neubauer maintained that his top *Rennfahrer* had "over-normal sight". Like binocular lenses his eyes let in more light, so he could see through cloud-bursts with a sort of visual radar. Neubauer relates that Caracciola never really "learned" to drive; it was a natural instinctive talent and he just "felt it".

Apparently Rudolf Caracciola "felt it" very keenly that wet August day in Ireland, for the world was his that day and all the might of the assembled Bentleys, Bugattis, and Alfa-Romeos could not deprive him of first place. There would be other days of glory: at Klausenpass, at Semmering, the Irish Grand Prix next year in an SSK, and even the arrogant Mille Miglia the year after. But there was something special about that day at Ards. Old Irishmen still speak of it with awe, and for visitors who will listen there are tales of a ghostly white machine that still runs those roads on moonless nights.

Ferdinand Porsche did not watch many of Caracciola's spectacular successes achieved with the cars from his drawing office in Stuttgart. In pretty little cafes over steaming cups of *Kaffee mit Schlag* and spicy slices of Sacher torte, the Viennese promise themselves they will never fall victim to a peculiarly German malady which roughly translates as "business manager's sickness". By 1928, Porsche had had enough of the "big town" to nearly qualify him for a good case, so he prudently went home to Austria and to work for the Steyr Works. Ironically, he left the pièce de résistance of his work, the potent 300 HP 156 MPH SSKL, to his successor Hans Nibel. He probably couldn't have cared less, for those cars were behind him, boring and unchallenging. Daimler-Benz would hear of him again in a few years, when

An "SS" (Super Sport) of 1928 with 7.1 litre supercharged engine. Only 111 cars were built (1928–1933) at a chassis cost of $10,800 to $12,100. (*Courtesy, Daimler-Benz*)

The 370 S Mannheim Sports of 1929 had lines suggestive of the more powerful and expensive "S" series Mercedes-Benz cars, but can be quickly distinguished by its flat Benz-style radiator. (Courtesy, Daimler-Benz)

The 370 S Mannheim sports was developed from a prosaic 3.1 litre touring car by Hans Nibel. It featured an L-head engine, six-speed gearbox, two-speed vacuum-operated rear, and straight through exhaust system. (*Courtesy, Daimler-Benz*)

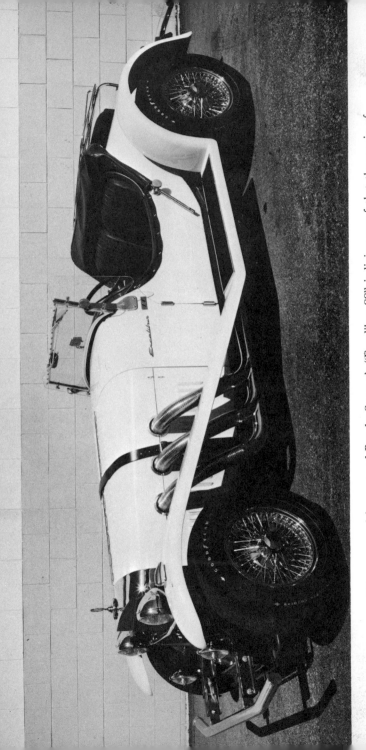

The commercial success of Brooks Stevens's "Excalibur SS" is living proof that the magic of the "S" series Mercedes-Benz has come down through the years untarnished. Built of modern American components, this SSK replica offers the same sort of brutal, exhilarating performance as its namesake. (*Courtesy, SS Automobiles, Inc.*)

he designed the formidable rear-engined Auto-Union racers which, with Mercedes-Benz Grand Prix cars, were Grand Prix racing in the later 1930s. The world would hear of him again, too, as father of the Volkswagen and its hot-rod offspring which still carries his name with consummate pride.

*Chapter* **6**

# The Great Grand
# Touring Era

Many of the grand marques of motor history—
Bugatti, Bentley, Hispano-Suiza, Rolls-Royce, and Duesenberg—are traceable to the personal talents of single, inspired individuals. Whether it was a Fred Duesenberg toil-
ing with his own oily hands in a rented garage in New
Jersey or Ettore Bugatti directing a feudal fief in Alsace,
their cars were highly personal extensions of themselves. It
was a rare sort of individualism, but not a very enduring
arrangement. In Bugatti's case it was, "Le Patron est mort,
la voiture est mort aussi", and most such cars—to the
world's loss—have passed on with their creators.

From its beginning way back in 1886, old Gottlieb Daimler's company seems to have been blessed with an unusual
ability to mobilize design talent without stripping men of
their individual imprint on the great cars that have carried
the name *Mercedes*. Over the years Mercedes cars have been
consistently "Mercedes-ish". Yet, the original Mercedes was
thoroughly Wilhelm Maybach in concept; Paul Daimler's
pre-World War I Grand Prix and high performance cars

were purely his own; and who else but Ferdinand Porsche could have fathered the screaming supercharged sports cars of the twenties? In 1929, Porsche was succeeded as Daimler-Benz's Chief Engineer by another individualist named Hans Nibel. His imprint on Mercedes-Benz was boldly personal and dramatic, and it endures today on the newest Mercedes you can buy.

Hans Nibel had come to *Benz und Cie* as a promising young designer back in the heroic days of racing. His first assignment was the 1908 Benz Grand Prix car which proved formidable competition for Mercedes racers, and he later developed that car into the 21.5 litre, 142 MPH "Blitzen Benz". In 1923, Nibel built a very fascinating racing machine which was far ahead of its time. Bizarre and extremely aerodynamic, the Benz two-litre literally looked like a bomb on wheels, and its unconventionality was more than skin deep. An early exponent of rear engine design, Nibel had moved the six-cylinder, double-overhead cam, roller-bearing engine back over the rear axle and placed the radiator in a cowl-like construction behind the driver's head. That rear axle under the engine was worth close inspection because it was a floating axle providing independent rear suspension for Nibel's racer and a "laboratory" for future experiments with springing.

When Hans Nibel succeeded to the hallowed Porsche drawing board at Stuttgart, he found himself with the task of improving the grandest sports car in the world, the fast and fearsome SSK Mercedes-Benz. The "S" series cars had gone through intense improvement and development under Ferdinand Porsche's genius, and an analytical look at the 225 HP arrogantly elegant machine did not suggest immediate improvement. However, Nibel answered the challenge with the daring use of the famous "Elephant blower" which fed twelve pounds of pressure through the twin carburetors

Picking up Porsche's concept of the big, fire-breathing sports car, Hans Nibel fitted the SSK with the twelve-pound "Elephant Blower" and a high lift counter-balanced crankshaft, and then harked back to the old racing trick of punching holes in the frame to lighten the chassis. The result was the SSKL, and a top speed of 156 MPH. (*Courtesy, Daimler-Benz*)

The *Mille Miglia* has only twice been beaten by non-Italian drivers on non-Italian cars, both times on Mercedes-Benz. Here, Rudolf Caracciola in an SSKL, as developed by Hans Nibel from Dr. Porsche's precedents, roars through Raticosa Pass on his way to victory. (*Courtesy, Daimler-Benz*)

In 1923, while he was still Chief Engineer for *Benz und Cie*, Hans Nibel designed a very advanced racing car which combined aerodynamic bomb-like body, a six-cylinder, double overhead-cam, roller bearing engine, and a floating axle to provide independent rear suspension. (*Courtesy, Daimler-Benz*)

and howled like a demented demon. That, plus a special high-lift counterbalanced crankshaft, now put 300 HP at hand. To enliven things a little more, Nibel harked back to an old time racing trick of lightening the car by punching holes in the chassis until it looked like a piece of Swiss cheese. This car added the final and rarest letter of the "letter cars", "L" for *leicht* (light), to create the SSKL.

Nibel's esoteric machine was never offered for sale to the public. It remained a works car and was used to write some scarlet pages in racing history in the early thirties. A stream-lined version was used by Manfred von Brauchitsch to hit 156 MPH at the Avus track near Berlin, and in 1931–32 the SSKL added twenty-eight major victories to the Daimler-Benz record books. By far the greatest of these was Rudolf Caracciola's Herculean mastery of the *Mille Miglia*. This extremely challenging race had been started in 1927 and was custom tailored to Italian cars and drivers. The course covered a thousand complex miles in the heart of Italy from Brescia to Rome and back over mountains and curves where the road holding finesse and understeer of spritely Italian cars were a strong asset. In the twenty-three years that the *Mille Miglia* was run it is noteworthy that non-Italian cars and drivers beat it only twice. Caracciola had run the course in 1930 in an SSK and his sixth place finish was very respectable. Now, the ultimate SSKL on its maiden voyage would be thrown against the Italian challenge.

The cars left Brescia early on the morning of the 12th of April and Caracciola immediately began to set up fantastic averages which were sometimes near Sterling Moss's times twenty-four years later in his 300 SLR. Down the Adriatic Coast, almost flat out all the way, then across toward Rome, and north through Florence, and on to Brescia—the supercharged 7.1 litres screaming defiance all the way. Sixteen hours and ten minutes after he left, Rudolf Caracciola was back in Brescia. Although a relief driver rode with him, he drove all the way himself in a dazzling feat of endurance.

The SSKL represented the classic bolide raised to its final form and to tamper with it further would have been sacrilege. So, leaning on the lessons learned from the "S" cars, Nibel turned his talents to developing a massive touring version based on a 7.7 litre, supercharged engine. This car inaugurated a concept which would come to be closely associated with Daimler-Benz—the all-out super luxury

Developed out of the concepts of the "S" cars, the first *Grosser Mercedes* of 1930 was an ultra VIP car. The Emperor of Japan bought seven of them between 1932 and 1935. Three still survive and are used as the official ceremonial car of the Japanese Imperial Family. The cars carry a gold chrysanthemum, the Imperial symbol, on the radiator. (*Courtesy, Daimler-Benz*)

"Grosser Mercedes". Not to be confused with the later, more svelte and technically sophisticated *Grosser* of 1938, the original 770K of 1930 was an enormously solid and staid car well suited to its usual ceremonial duties.

Today, the Japanese still find no complaint with the three surviving cars of the seven purchased by their Emperor in the 1930s. The 770 K Grosser Mercedes is still the official ceremonial car of the Japanese Imperial family, which uses its modern Rolls-Royces merely for everyday use. Despite the passage of thirty seven years the 770 K is still very "head-of-state" in bearing, just as Oliver Statler described it in *Japanese Inn*. "And then it came, the big Mercedes-Benz, a regal automobile with a regal disdain for fashion. Its angular black top loomed a foot higher than the submissively curved sedans that crawled behind, its maroon body was big and boxy. It bore the gold Chrysanthemum."

For a while, Hans Nibel followed the Porsche precedents at Stuttgart. But while Ferdinand Porsche's forte was basically engines, Nibel was an expert on springing and suspension and was interested in seeing that a car could go with maximum comfort and stability as well as speed. Thus, he began a period of experimentation in the early 1930s which led to some of the very finest Grand Touring cars ever built.

Nibel believed that a floating or swing axle, as he had used on his 1923 racer, offered the best advantages for independent wheel suspension. A French designer named Sensaud de Lavaud picked up the idea and developed it further but nothing really concrete was done until the little 170, the first independently sprung Mercedes-Benz, appeared in 1931. The 170 was simultaneously a proving ground and successful showpiece for Nibel's independent suspension theories. The 1.7 litre, six-cylinder car (later a four-cylinder), although not an inspiring performer, offered fine economy combined with an almost limousine-like ride and the prestige of a Mercedes-Benz star for under $2000. The 170 became a most successful money maker for Daimler-Benz; tens of thousands were sold through a variety of changes and updatings, and a direct descendant—the 170 S—was still in production in the early 1950s.

At the rear, the 170's box section tubular frame curved sharply upward to allow free movement of the swinging rear axle which worked in conjunction with coil springs. Up front, the wheels rode on a pair of transverse mounted leaf springs, a separate set above and below, completely without a conventional axle. In later models, coil springs were substituted for the leaf arrangement.

As early as 1927, Daimler-Benz was experimenting with a

In the later twenties, Daimler-Benz began to develop a Volkswagen-like rear engined car called the 130 H (*Heckmotor*, rear engine). In 1936, an improved 1.7-litre model was offered as a companion to the more conventional 170, but the "Mercedes-Benz beetle" never really caught on. (*Courtesy, Daimler-Benz*)

Cabriolet version of the 170 H, obvious ancestor of and inspiration for Dr. Porsche's Volkswagen. (*Courtesy, Daimler-Benz*)

swing axle rear engined car which used a 1.3 litre four-cylinder, air-cooled, horizontally-opposed engine. The 130H (*Heckmotor*, rear engine) was somewhat timidly introduced in the wake of the more conventional 170 front-engined car, and was the obvious inspiration for Dr. Porsche's Volkswagen a few years later. A subsequent 170H was shown in 1936 but apparently the world was not quite ready for a "Mercedes-Benz beetle".

Nibel's suspension provided hitherto unexperienced comfort in a small car, and increased control and roadability on rough surfaces was a very definite safety factor. With characteristic Daimler thoroughness, the new idea was developed and expanded into the two-litre "200", and in 1932 the advanced suspension system was first adapted to a sports car, the supercharged 3.8 litre, eight-cylinder "380" Mercedes-Benz. This was a stylishly elegant sports/luxury machine of flowing lines which offered a prediction of things to come.

The 1932 Salon de Paris was the setting for the unveiling of an epic Mercedes-Benz and a milestone in motoring history. The lithe new 500K was a classic combination of taste and technical talent which, for all the attempts, appears only rarely. The chassis was a distillation of the Daimler foray into the field of advanced suspension. Swing axles were, of course, *de rigeur*, with a separate universal joint for each half of the axle and two big coil springs for each rear wheel. The independent front suspension system was built around wishbone arms attached to the rugged H-section frame. Single coil springs were used for the front wheels.

Into this chassis was laid a straight-eight, five-litre engine developed out of the 380 which could develop a hundred horsepower and high torque at fairly low revolutions. It

Chassis layout of the 170 H Mercedes-Benz which laid down most of the concepts for the Volkswagen which Dr. Porsche developed a few years later as the famous "peoples' car." (*Courtesy, Daimler-Benz*)

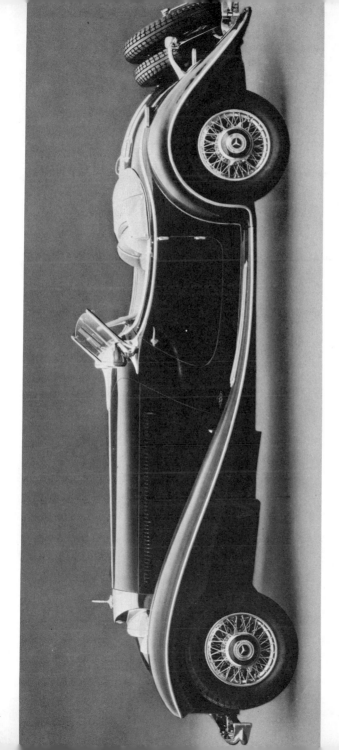

The brightest glint of a golden age: the 500 K Mercedes-Benz sports roadster. (*Courtesy, Daimler-Benz*)

The world's first successful Diesel passenger car, the 260 D Mercedes-Benz, appeared in 1936

540 K "A" type cabriolet is one of the most popularly restored classic cars. Besides being a showpiece, it can give modern performance on the highway. (*Photograph by the author*)

was a quiet and reliable pushrod, overhead-valve engine running on nine main bearings, but the addition of the letter "K" for *Kompressor*, or supercharger, changed it into a screaming siren straight out of Wagner. Like the blowers on the old "S" cars, the 500K's supercharger cut in "on demand" when the accelerator was floored. The power output jumped from 100 H.P. to 160 H.P. and nearly three tons of steel and high style were smartly propelled to a top speed of over 100 MPH.

To suitably tailor the 500K chassis, Daimler-Benz turned to its own coachbuilding works at Sindelfingen. The factory catalogue offered seven "standard" models of the 500K which included jaunty tourers, charming cabriolets (the usual medium of expression), and closed models. But the unchallenged star of the show was a ravishing sports roadster which would have done credit to the most elite bespoke coachbuilder of Paris or London.

For this gem, the artists at Sindelfingen had reached into the stratosphere of automotive art to create a truly timeless car. Preserving the arrogant elegance of the older "S" cars, they added the suave influence of flowing lines to fashion a car that can still stop traffic at any intersection in the civilized world. The imperious Vee radiator, wedge-shaped windscreen, gracefully curved fenders, triple-laced wire wheels, and dashing rear-mounted twin spares were a visual symphony of motoring excitement. Inside were fine wide seats of fragrant leather for two, a fully instrumented dash panel of choice rubbed walnut with matching door trim, and a solid sense of security at speed which only a Mercedes-Benz could provide. The 500K had enormous cachet and psychological appeal; in the author's opinion even more than its successor 540K. In a sense, the 500K sports roadster seemed a summing up point for automobiles in general and Mercedes-Benz in particular; perhaps it was the brightest glint of a golden age.

It is a sad thing that Dr. Nibel did not live to see a few more of his ideas come to full fruition. His post was taken over in 1935 by Max Sailer, a multi-talented man who had given so much to Mercedes on race circuits from the 1914 French Grand Prix to his gallant drive in the 1921 Targa Florio. A good bit of diversified activity was going on in Stuttgart-Unterturkheim under Sailer's reign. Grand Prix racing had, of course, started up again, a pair of somewhat less grand touring cars—the 230 and 320—were being developed, and an interesting Diesel car project was under way.

With the aid of Bosch fuel injection pumps, Sailer solved the problem of making a Diesel engine a practical proposition for a private car. The 2.6 litre "260 D" with its 45 HP at 3000 RPM and 60 MPH top speed would never be a track star, but it offered economy, utility, and fantastic durability. Daimler-Benz still likes to tell the story of one 260 D which served its Wurttemberg owner through thirteen years and 808,000 miles, some of them pulling an oversized trailer in wartime.

The 1936 Mercedes-Benz catalogue described the new 540K as "an international conception of beauty and speed". Basically, the car was a reworked version of the 500K with a slight displacement increase giving 115 HP for normal driving and 180 HP with the supercharger going. Performance went up; zero to fifty in ten seconds with three tons of unabashed luxury underneath you was not at all bad for 1936. The 540K gave the firm impression that there was nothing less than a battleship under you, and the straight-eight engine was an untemperamental workhorse of a thing that would cruise at ninety from dawn to dark without raising a sweat (2700 RPM at 90 MPH). Its overbuilt Teutonic staunchness assured that it would continue to do so for some time to come. Mr. M. L. Cohn of Los Angeles, a vintage director of the Mercedes-Benz Club of America, owns a 540K with something over 200,000 miles on the clock. The car still runs like a $500 watch without ever having had the cylinder head removed.

Again, seven styles of coachwork "out of the book" were available on the 540K chassis, and again the sports roadster was the most electrifying. The basic concept of the 500K sports was fortunately preserved, but updated and streamlined. On the 500K, the non-padded top folded nearly into the coachwork and was covered with a canvas boot, while on the 540K roadster the top disappeared completely into the body and a hinged metal panel snapped over it. There was a little more chrome, and the rear-mounted spares now

A non-stock version of the 540 K sports roadster which retains the sporty, old-style, exposed rear-mounted spare. (*Courtesy, Daimler-Benz*)

hid in an interior compartment. With its narrow Vee wind-screen, wide curved fenders, and cozy cockpit the whole car seemed to take on a distinctly aeronautical flavor.

The 500K and 540K cars were not without their critics. The usual critique was that they did not measure up to their illustrious ancestors the "S" cars and that they were soft and over-civilized. The "S" machines *were* an imposing criterion, but it seems quite unfair to compare the two cars since they represent rather different concepts. The "S" cars were, for the most part, all-out sports machines and were among the two or three sports cars in history that could be raced as full fledged Grand Prix machinery. On the other hand, the 500K and 540K were devised as comfortable, safe, and quite elegant means of getting from point A to point B, especially if there was a good deal of distance in between. They were, in essence, early and rather good examples of the *Gran Turismo* car, or what Detroit people now call the "personal luxury car."

The 500 K and 540 K were predominantly open cars and many were done as cabriolets with big, heavily padded tops. That great assemblage of bows, horsehair padding, and fabric which rested behind the passenger compartment when the top was down offended some, particularly the English. One prominent British motoring writer called the arrangement "hideous in the worst Teutonic way." It is a matter of personal taste. The author has always rather fancied the elegant, carriage-like look, and it cannot be denied that the cabriolet construction had a secure German substantiality about it that offered the only way of building an open car that was structurally as safe as a closed one. Some time ago the author owned a Mercedes-Benz which had been less than skillfully cornered at around 80 MPH. The effect on a modern convertible would have been thermonuclear, but that big old top (ten years old at the time) yielded only a

Mercedes-Benz 540 K "B" type five passenger cabriolet. Despite great weight, a 540 K could accelerate from zero to fifty in ten seconds, and had a top speed of about 110 MPH. In all, 406 540 Ks were built. (*Courtesy, Daimler-Benz*)

With its narrow Vee windscreen, wide curved fenders, cozy cockpit, and sleek, lithe lines the 540 K sports roadster took on a distinctly aeronautical flavor. (*Courtesy, Daimler-Benz*)

The arrogant elegance of the 540 K sports roadster of 1936. (*Courtesy, Daimler-Benz.*)

few inches to one side and a couple layers of fabric. The driver was disciplined mainly with a black eye.

In 1938, time was running out for Mercedes-Benz automobiles; indeed, for most of the world. By then a large part of production had been appropriated by the military, four hundred specialists were devoted to dominating international Grand Prix racing, and normal production of cars and trucks was being pushed. In the midst of this, time was found to update the *Grosser* Mercedes to the technical level of the 540K, using a lower tubular chassis, swing axles and coil springs, and a five speed synchromesh gearbox. In Daimler-Benz's own words the new 770K was designed "for those who desired a car which was quite outside the ordinary run of things." It was that, all right, and to get one you had to be quite outside the ordinary run of people. Sharing a distinction with only one other car, the Phantom IV Rolls-Royce, the 770K was never offered for sale to the general public and often ended up in garages of people like Premier Salazar of Portugal or Field Marshal Mannerheim

Mercedes-Benz 540 K A type cabriolet, 1936–1939. (*Courtesy, Daimler-Benz*)

770 K cabriolet without the third, rear quarter window afforded more privacy for the passengers. Fully outfitted and fueled, a 770 K weighed approximately 10,000 pounds. (*Courtesy, Daimler-Benz*)

In 1938, Daimler-Benz revised the 770 K *Grosser* Mercedes to bring it up to the technical level of the 540 K. Only eighteen of the "super" cars were made, and were never offered for sale to the general public. (*Courtesy, Daimler-Benz*)

A 770 K in a characteristic pose; top down, windows up. Even with armor plating and 1¾-inch-thick glass the car would still top 100 MPH. (*Courtesy, Daimler-Benz*)

of Finland. Most of the eighty-eight 770Ks built found their way into the hands of the Nazi hierarchy.

Lord Montagu's Motor Museum at Beaulieu has a 770K formerly used by Herman Goering which may be considered as typical of its kind. It is a seven seater cabriolet (a less imposing closed version was also made) which, with armor plating and 1¾-inch-thick bullet proof glass, weighs 10,000 pounds. With that kind of weight and over twenty feet of non-aerodynamic coachwork, the 770K did not set any acceleration records—even with the supercharger going —although it could top 100 MPH if you had enough straight in front of you.

*Chapter* 7

# The Silver Star
# At Speed

It dishonors no great racing marque, past or present, to say that Mercedes-Benz has been the most consistently successful participant in automobile racing. Alfa-Romeo, Bentley, Bugatti, Ferrari, and Maserati have all had fabulous flings of success—some of them rather heady. But Daimler-Benz racing record books go all the way back to 1894 when a Daimler engine powered the winning car of the Paris-Rouen. And in the following three quarters of a century, those books have seen the entry of some four thousand bright moments on road and track.

Certainly the most absolute and overwhelming victories ever recorded anywhere fell to the Mercedes-Benz racing team in the middle 1930s. It was a time when the silver star at speed was at its zenith. Mercedes-Benz drivers were no longer merely instructed to win—they were told in what order they should cross the finish line. The cars themselves ignored and defied all manner of convention and eventually rose to represent what no lesser authority than Laurence Pomeroy called "the peak development of the piston engine." One car, the W125, unleashed 646 HP from a 5.6 litre engine and had a power-to-weight ratio even lower than that of contemporary Daimler-Benz aircraft engines. Such cars were not easily driven. By way of comparison, it has been said that an ordinary "good driver" behind the wheel would feel as if he were driving on glazed ice and doing 100 MPH.

Since Daimler-Benz had fielded its last all-out Grand Prix car in 1925, Bugatti, Alfa-Romeo, and a promising new-comer, the Brothers Maserati, had developed and run some fast, efficient Grand Prix machinery. Despite a case of the Depression doldrums, development was pushed to a point at which by 1934 the Association Internationale des Automobiles-Clubs had become concerned about the 150 MPH upper speed range of these cars. So, for the 1934 season they announced a new Grand Prix formula calcu-lated to miniaturize both the cars and their speeds. While there were no direct restrictions on engine size or output, the Association decreed that the weight of the car (not including oil, gas, water, and tires) could not exceed 750 kilograms, or 1624 pounds. Despite minor restrictions on width, entrants were free to do what they wanted as long as they stayed inside 750 kilograms.

What the Association envisioned was a crop of small, lightweight, and—hopefully—slower cars with an average displacement of about two and a half liters. They certainly did not suspect anything like what Messrs. Nibel, Sailer, Wagner, Neubauer, and Uhlenhaut were about to cook up on the back burner at the far end of the Daimler-Benz works at Stuttgart.

When Mercedes-Benz decided to get back into Grand Prix racing for the 1934 season under the new 750 kg formula, it began an era of half a dozen years which was to be unlike anything else in the annals of auto racing, before

In 1936, the job of developing a new racing car was turned over to Rudolph Uhlenhaut who responded with the 646 HP W 125. (*Courtesy, Daimler-Benz*)

When Mercedes-Benz entered Grand Prix racing in 1934 under the new 750 kg formula, its first car was the W 125, a 3.36 to 4-litre car of 354 HP which could reach 200 MPH in less than a mile. Above, the winning car in the 1934 Italian Grand Prix driven alternately by Caracciola and Fagioli. (*Courtesy, Daimler-Benz*)

or since. The German government, anxious to see German cars again in the lead, decided to get into the act by offering a $100,000 grant which was awarded to Daimler-Benz and used to develop the 1934 Grand Prix car. Rather much has been made of this grant-in-aid business. Certainly, the politicians got their money's worth in propaganda value, and the cash was useful. But, even though it did increase as time went on, it was never sufficient to underwrite or entirely finance the Grand Prix program. At its height, the Racing

Department at Stuttgart employed four hundred highly skilled specialists whose salaries alone came to many times the amount of the grants. The money made things easier, but it is doubtful if the final story would have been much different without it.

The first car of the Mercedes-Benz Grand Prix series, the *Werksnummer 25*, started right out by making a shambles of the 750 kg formula. Hans Nibel's experimental department responded to the challenge with a 3.36 litre, eight-cylinder, double overhead-camshaft engine of incredible lightness and efficiency. Fitted with a front mounted supercharger and two pressure carburetors, the W25 put out some 354 HP and in final drive was good for 200 MPH in

Caracciola and von Brauchitsch take a curve at the 1937 Grand Prix de Monaco in their W 125s. Mercedes took the first three places at Monaco that year, plus five other Grand Prix victories. (*Courtesy, Daimler-Benz*)

less than a mile. Such raw power was at best of limited use and at worst outright deadly if the chassis could not handle it. This was, succinctly, the very situation which had brought about the 750 kg formula in the first place—cars that could dangerously outrun their chassis. However, Nibel was, of course, the industry's past master on springing and suspension. He proceeded to adapt his swing axle concepts to racing technique. The result was a completely independently sprung Grand Prix racing machine capable of maintaining contact with the road at all times. Even Nibel could not claim it to be easy to drive, but it was thoroughly tractable even in the upper speed range.

The new W25 represented the very last word in modern racing car design, but perhaps the most amazing thing of all about it was that the car had been conceived, designed, built, and tested within about nine months. The car had its running-in problems but, all things considered, the W25 was nothing short of a mini-miracle.

One of these teething troubles came at the W25's maiden outing at the Eifelrennen at Nurburgring in June of 1934 and proved both amusing and historic. At the official inspection and weigh-in the shiny German racing white Mercedes-Benz weighed exactly one kilogram over the limit! Relating the story years later, Rudolf Uhlenhaut recalls that the white paint had been laid on in a "rather thick coating to make the panels nice and even. We had to scrape all this nice paint off, which had cost a lot of money, a lot of time; and we had to expose the blank aluminum. We got off quite a lot of pounds and the car was inside the limits. From that time on our cars weren't painted any more. They had this well known aluminum color."

The aluminum color became famous and Mercedes-Benz racers of the period were sometimes nicknamed "Silver Arrows". Naked of paint, the W25 went on to win the Eifelrennen. Uhlenhaut tells an interesting sequel. After another race, the officials decided to re-weigh all cars to be sure that nothing had been bolted on that didn't belong. Again the W25 turned up a few pounds heavy. Since the 750 kg limit was dry weight, the Mercedes-Benz team promptly disassembled all parts that ran in oil and wiped them off. Dry, the car just met the weight limit. Uhlenlaut laughed and called it "quite a narrow affair".

Within a month after its debut, an improved 3.71 litre version of the W25 was ready and running. And before the year was out, another four litre model putting up 430 HP was in use. In its inaugural year, the W25 did respectably well for itself with five wins and three second places. Later, it rounded off the year by setting two interesting records which served notice on unconvinced competitors of just what they were up against. The first record attempt was run on the Gyon course near Budapest where a W25 was started from rest and within a mile was traveling at 199.36 MPH. A similar run at Avus on the 10th of December, 1934, was set up for the flying mile and yielded 193.85 MPH.

Under the 750 kg formula the improved version of the W25 laid down repeated victories for Mercedes-Benz in 1935–36. Except for the big rear-engined Porsche-designed Auto Unions—which were also receiving government grants—serious competition for the Silver Arrows had all but evaporated. The last fling of other cars came at the 1935 German Grand Prix where the great Italian ace, Tazio Nuvolari, in an Alfa-Romeo set up a classic hounding of Manfred von Brauchitsch on his W25. By the last few laps the crowd's excitement was at a fever pitch, as both men seemed equally determined not to yield to the other. Von Brauchitsch would not even go in for a much needed tire change, so close was the half-minute margin between him and the Italian, and he decided to risk the last two laps on his balding right rear tire. It was a magnificent match of man against machine; Nuvolari's gallant Alfa-Romeo was vastly overmatched and he was fighting the big Mercedes-Benz with pure skill 'and daring alone. Then, at almost the last permissible second, von Brauchitsch's tire blew and—Viva Italia!—Nuvolari swept past to win the German Grand Prix.

A brief look at Mercedes's hot competition, the Porsche-designed Auto Union racers, is valuable here. They were sometimes the only adversaries, but were always worthy, interesting, competitors. The year before the 750 kg formula went into effect, four of Germany's important auto builders (Audi, DKW, Horch, and Wanderer) had merged to form Auto Union and had adopted four interlocking rings as their symbol. The new company decided to get in on the German government's program of offering cash grants to stimulate successful international competition cars. Wisely, it turned for expertise to Dr. Ferdinand Porsche who was conveniently already at work on a novel racing car project. Porsche's efforts were adopted almost intact, and Porsche now worked in concert with Eberan von Eberhorst.

The first Auto Union designed to comply with the 750 kg formula, the A-type, was a rear engined automobile powered by a V-16, 4.36 litre engine turning out 295 HP at 4500 RPM. Following Mercedes-Benz precedent, there was independent suspension provided by swing axle construction. In their first year of racing, the A-type Auto Unions were quite successful, taking three major races to Mercedes-Benz's four. The Auto Unions went through two additional versions and in final form were good for over 500 HP and 200 MPH. The Auto Union team consisted of some superb driving talent, but none greater than the memorable Bernd

W 125s at speed in the German Grand Prix of 1937. The W 125 had such acceleration that

Rosemeyer who handled the difficult Auto Unions with consummate finesse and was always an on-track threat to Mercedes-Benz. Rosemeyer was killed in an Auto Union early in 1938 while trying to beat a record run of 268.3 MPH set by Rudolf Caracciola in a Mercedes-Benz.

Although the 750 kg formula was carried over for the 1937 season, Daimler-Benz felt that the W25 had done its duty and decided to field a new racing car for 1937. The project was dumped into the lap of a man both capable and worthy of it, Rudolf Uhlenhaut. Half English and half German, Uhlenhaut represents a rare and successful blend of English patience and perseverance and German inventiveness and attention to detail. Uhlenhaut came to Daimler-Benz in 1931, took over the racing experiments in 1936, later became a director, and today is the world's most eminent automobile designer with the world's most advanced passenger car, the 300 SEL 6.3 litre Mercedes-Benz, to his credit.

With the same precision with which he speaks a flawless, British-flavored English, Uhlenhaut set out to build a new racing car. Self effacingly, he recalls that at the time he "hadn't any real idea about racing cars", and so he took two W25s to the Nurburgring and learned to drive them. After 2500 miles, he had "used up" the cars and had formed some opinions about what should go into the successor car, the W125. One of these was that it would be possible to build a big 5.66 litre engine to throw off over 646 HP and still stay within the 750 kg dry-weight restriction. Development of what promised to be the most remarkable car of that, or any other, age went forward with typical German thoroughness. All development was done on special test benches, and only then was a complete engine built and tested. The same procedure was followed for the axles and suspension and

W 125s with streamlined coachwork in the International Avus race, July 25, 1937. In 1938, Rudolf Caracciola drove a similar aerodynamic car at a record 268.9 MPH. (*Courtesy, Daimler-Benz*)

even for the gas tanks which were tested with a "thorough shaking" on a machine resembling an oversized paint mixer.

When science and theory had been exhausted, the new *Werksnummer 125* was sent to Nurburgring for that final kind of testing that cannot be computed ahead of time. It was Uhlenhaut's concept that if you relied solely on your drivers' capabilities to win races, no matter how good they were, you were in trouble. He felt that a driver was reasonably safe only if he could drive within a prescribed limit, "and that he could only do if his car is superior to his competitor's." It was Uhlenhaut's duty to provide such a car. The tests at Nurburgring strongly suggested that that was exactly what he had done in creating the W125.

Despite the addition of about 250 fresh horsepower, the W125 handled better than the 400 HP W25 thanks to vastly improved power transmission and suspension. Again, Mercedes-Benz passenger car suspension had supplied the inspiration, but this time with a new twist. Daimler-Benz officially describes the suspension of the W125: "The independent front suspension with open coil springs was similar to model 500K and 540K. The method of controlling the thrust of the rear wheels was, however, entirely new. It was a special construction which ensured that the rear wheels kept in track and that the thrust and braking momentum was transmitted to the frame of the car through guides mounted on the side. The driving axles with universal joints were not enclosed, and torsion bars were used for the rear suspension." All of this was carried on an incredibly strong oval tubular frame of chrome molybdenum steel of only 1.5 mm thickness which was so light that it could be picked up by one man.

Stated simply, the W125 was a car with a superabundance of power which, significantly, could be controlled. The acceleration of the car was prodigious. The most striking example of it, as originally cited by George Monkhouse who spent part of a racing season with the Mercedes-Benz team, was that if a W125 was standing still and just started to move as it was passed by a car doing 100 MPH it would catch and pass that car *within a mile!* Even at 150 MPH the W125 could spin wheels and burn rubber if the accelerator was suddenly floored. Monkhouse records that prepping for the Grand Prix of Tripoli in 1937 the W125 took "a large number of corners practically flat out at 180 MPH."

The W125 produced a good return on its investment for the 1937 season, which is most easily recounted by the following chart:

| Date | Race | Driver |
|------|------|--------|
| 9th May | Grand Prix of Tripoli (first place) | Lang |
| 25th July | Grand Prix of Germany (first & second) | Caracciola |
| 8th August | Grand Prix of Monaco (first, second, & third) | von Brauchitsch |
| 22nd August | Grand Prix of Switzerland (first, second, third, & fourth) | Caracciola |
| 12th September | Grand Prix of Italy (first place) | Caracciola |
| 26th September | Grand Prix of Czechoslovakia (first & second) | Caracciola |

A final pièce de résistance was added in January of 1938 when a special streamlined version of the W125 was rolled out onto the Autobahn between Frankfort and Darmstadt.

Rudolf Caracciola climbed in and drove the car 271.5 MPH over the flying kilometer.

By 1938, the Association Internationale des Automobiles-Clubs finally realized that Daimler-Benz had effectively de-fanged their formula of 750 kg, and so they announced a new one for the 1938 season. The new formula raised the weight limit to 850 kilograms with tires (1874 pounds) but now specified that a supercharged engine could not displace over three litres and an unsupercharged engine four and a half litres. The engineers at Stuttgart met the new challenge without a blink and obediently devised the *Werksnummer* 154.

Although the W154 preserved the splendid suspension of the W125, it was otherwise quite a different machine. To compensate for the displacement decrease, designers went up to a V-12 engine using four overhead camshafts, nine oil pumps, and a two-stage, twenty-seven-pound-pressure supercharger. The engine was capable of 7800 RPM and a little over 480 HP. The W154 also *looked* quite different from its ancestors. It had such a startlingly low center of gravity that the driver sat a scant six inches off the road. A very low, wide, and streamlined look was accomplished by mounting the engine diagonally and using an offset drive shaft which rode next to the driver on his left side rather than under him.

The W154 was good evidence that the Daimler-Benz Grand Prix car technique was becoming more sophisticated wih each edition. It handled better than the preceding cars, had improved brakes and softer suspension, and could set up equal times despite a loss of about 170 HP. An improved but similar version of the W154 was also built and called the W163. Together, they added some interesting reading to the Daimler-Benz record books, again best summarized in chart form:

| Date | Race | Driver |
|---|---|---|
| 15th May, 1938 | Grand Prix of Tripoli (first, second, & third) | Lang |
| 3rd July, 1938 | Grand Prix of France (first, second, & third) | von Brauchitsch |
| 24th July, 1938 | Grand Prix of Germany (first & second) | Seaman |
| 21st August, 1938 | Grand Prix of Switzerland (first, second, & third) | Caracciola |
| 8th April, 1939 | Grand Prix of Pau (first & second) | Lang |
| 21st May, 1939 | International Eifel Races (first, third, & fourth) | Lang |
| 25th June, 1939 | Grand Prix of Belgium (first & third) | Lang |
| 23rd July, 1939 | Grand Prix of Germany (first place) | Caracciola |
| 20th August, 1939 | Grand Prix of Switzerland (first, second, & third) | Lang |

The Mercedes sweep of the circuits was not calculated to make friends among the makers of racing cars. The Italians were particularly irritated over having their red cars swept into oblivion, and decided to do something about it in 1939. A neat little conspiracy was engineered to hand over the 1939 Tripoli Grand Prix to the Italians by restricting entrants to one and a half litres displacement, a class in which Italy was strong with Alfa-Romeo and Maserati. Word of this was kept from Mercedes and the world until the last possible moment. Apparently, some German James Bond was on the job, however, for Daimler's got word of the plan and the experimental department swung into action to create an entirely new racing car in less than eight months.

In 1947, Don Lee drove a W 163 at Indianapolis. Without the Mercedes pit work it was accustomed to, performance was not up to par and the car tended to overheat at high speed. The W 163's low slung silhouette was startlingly new for 1938 and was accomplished by an offset drive shaft and diagonally mounted engine. (*Courtesy, Indianapolis Motor Speedway*)

The fruit of the effort was the W165, a jewel-like, little 1.5 litre V-8 which could turn over 8250 RPM and over 250 HP. Much to Roman dismay, a pair of them showed up at Tripoli in May, and with Herman Lang and Rudolf Caracciola driving romped home easily to a one-two win at speeds only a few miles per hour lower than the W163, with double the displacement, had set up the year before.

The little W165, which ran only once, was the last of its kind. Although W163s were still winning races as late as August and September of 1939, an era had ended that May afternoon in North Africa. There was, however, one more car in the Daimler-Benz experimental department that never ran on anything beyond a slide rule. This was the fantastic record car, the T80, powered by a V-12, 44.5 litre, fuel-injected aircraft engine of some 3000 horsepower. The T80 was a fascinating exercise in high speed design with some points which are still modern today. It was a six-wheeler with power being supplied from a rear mounted four wheel "truck". An ingenious mechanism automatically cut power if rear wheel spin developed by cutting off the fuel supply to the injection system. Today, the T80 is a high point of the tour of the Daimler-Benz Museum at Stuttgart where a visitor can pause and wonder if the slide rule experts were right who said it would do exactly 404 MPH.

Men like Rudolf Uhlenhaut and his racing team manager, Alfred Neubauer, would be the first to admit that there is no such thing as an invincible racing organization. But Mercedes-Benz came closer to it in the period 1934–1939 than anyone else ever has.

How they did it was often as impressive as the machines they did it with. The "secret weapon" was not so much the abundant resources of Daimler-Benz as it was the intense, almost fanatical, thoroughness with which they were deployed. The sacrosanct Racing Department at Stuttgart was probably the nearest thing to a Cape Kennedy complex in existence at the time, and was about as easy to get into. One of the few outsiders who did get in was George Monkhouse who spent part of the 1937 season with the Mercedes-Benz Racing Team. There he found every conceivable piece of machinery, equipment, and gadget for testing and analyzing every part of an automobile, including an atmospherically controlled room which could duplicate the climate of any place on earth which had roads. Monkhouse was especially awed by the nerve center of the Experimental Department, Rudolf Uhlenhaut's office. He wrote: "In Uhlenhaut's office, pinned upon a drawing board, was a large map of the Donington circuit, on which all the gradients and radii of the curves had been measured off. This is merely an example of the thoroughness of the racing department, which enables them to prepare their cars, especially with regard to the correct gear ratios, for a new circuit without ever having seen it." (Used with permission; Floyd Clymer Publications, 2125 West Pico Blvd., Los Angeles, California 90006.)

Once a car left Uhlenhaut's province it became the personal concern of that arch organizer and perfectionist portly Alfred Neubauer. Under his firm hand, which combined the qualities of a favorite uncle and a Prussian general, the Mercedes-Benz racing team of the 1930s was the German penchant for preciseness given full reign. Grandiose legends have grown up about it. The more exotic ones are often true. Neatly uniformed technicians did march out to measure the temperature of the track, the tires, the atmosphere, and to record the barometric pressure. Engineers carefully calculated the angle of each curve, the rise of each grade. Meticulous assistants stood by with lacquered wooden cases packed with 1137 carburetor jets to cover any possible situation, even though the car had most likely been perfectly carbureted in the climate control room at Stuttgart. An expert from Bosch was sent out to inspect the spark plugs after practice runs and make selections for the race. The pit crews were tuned to concert pitch. In less than half a minute they could totally service an incoming car; supplying seventy-five gallons of gas, four tires, oil, clean windscreen, and a word of encouragement. One crewman once did it with his pants on fire, and anybody that determined deserves to win.

*Chapter* **8**

# The Star Rises Again

As one of the leading industrial complexes in Germany, Daimler-Benz was a prime target for Allied bombers in World War II. In the First World War, the company had suffered a lot of disruption but no actual physical damage; it was not so fortunate the second time around. In September of 1944, two weeks of daylight air raids left sixty years of Daimler and Benz history in smouldering ruins. The main plant at Stuttgart-Unterturkheim was listed as 70% destroyed; the vast aero engine and coach-building works nine miles away at Sindelfingen suffered 85% destruction; 80% of the truck works at Gaggenau was leveled; the original Benz und Cie site at Mannheim escaped with the least damage at 20%; the Berlin-Marienfeld works which Daimler bought in 1902 and later devoted to diesel and aero engines was totally bombed out.

Hardly more than a skeleton of Daimler-Benz Aktiengesellschaft survived the war. The Board of Directors issued a statement in which they declared that "Daimler-Benz had ceased to exist in 1945." Problems ranged from the obvious

The 300 C convertible limousine in diplomatic service, carrying Indian Prime Minister Nehru on a state visit. (*Courtesy, Daimler-Benz*)

financial ones to geographical, as the several plants were split up in different zones. For awhile it looked very much as if the world was about to lose the grandest of "the grand marques". But Gottlieb Daimler's and Karl Benz's ghosts prowled the rubble and inspired their successors to pick up the pieces and start over. Much of Daimler-Benz's intense sense of organization, and a good esprit de corps, survived the holocaust. Mechanic and executive alike cleared the debris, salvaged what little the bombers and looters missed, and started a modest program of vehicle repair and maintenance work. As early as 1946, production of the pre-war 170V was resumed but in the next two years less than six hundred were built. The valiant effort at reconstruction got a great shot in the arm from the currency reform and stabilization of 1948. The next year two re-designed versions, the 170S and 170D (Diesel), went into production and in 1949 well over 17,000 were built.

The 170 series were small, low powered cars and a far cry from the great 540K, but they were suitable for their austere post-war environment. Nevertheless, they had the experience of thousands of pre-war units to rely and build upon and they were technically fairly sophisticated automobiles for their kind. The 52 HP side-valve, 170S engine was nothing esoteric, to be sure, but it was durable, reliable, economical, and very well suited to its job. The suspension of the 170S had swing axles in the rear, of course, and the old transverse leaf spring independent front suspension was upgraded with wishbone and coil spring suspension according to 540K practice. The result was a solid, comfortable, and modestly performing little car with about a 75 MPH top speed. The author knows of one cabriolet model 170 S which lives not far away that is now on its second engine and into its nineteenth year of almost daily use and still serves with dignity and style.

Mercedes began its postwar production with the 170 series. Durable, economical, reliable, but comfortable, they were very suitable for their austere postwar environment. This little 170 cabriolet has seen nearly 19 years of daily use and still serves with dignity and style. *(Photograph by the author)*

The 170D was aimed even more at economy, and refined the lessons of the 1936 260D to cram over 40-miles-to-the-gallon frugality into a comfortable sedan. If you didn't mind taking three quarters of a minute to reach the maximum sixty miles an hour, the 170D was your dish of tea. Naturally, the 170D did a lot of utility duty, and a rather interesting version of it was developed for routine police patrol work. Officially designated the 170Da OTP (Offener Tourenwagen fur Polizei), these cars were open touring models fitted with the old folding cabriolet style top and had a certain elegance despite their business-like Polizei green or Bundeswehr brown. Recently, the 170Da OTP was phased out of civil service and cars were auctioned for

$50 to $75. Restored, some of them have shown up in this country at substantially higher prices.

The recovery of Daimler-Benz was no less than phenomenal. By 1951, the company was still no paragon of prosperity, but it was ready to step into a new era and re-affirm its traditional leadership on road and track. The Frankfurt Motor Show early in 1951 was chosen to introduce the two new models which were the first full efforts of the reconstructed engineering department. The 220 was partly an upgraded and luxurious expression of the 170, retaining the time proven suspension system and the basic classic lines, but under the hood the prosaic little side-valve four-cylinder had given way to an advanced 2.2 litre six-cylinder, overhead-camshaft engine of 80 HP and 90 MPH. The new 220

An interesting variation, the 170 Da OTP (open touring car for police) with Diesel engine. Many of these cars, obtained inexpensively as surplus in Germany, are being restored as classics. (*Photograph by the author*)

Dr. Fritz Nallinger and the 300 which he labored long and hard to make the most technically sophisticated luxury car of its day. Many of its features are still modern today. (*Courtesy, Daimler-Benz*)

combined lively performance with an almost sports car roadability.

The 300 luxury sedan which appeared along with the 220 was something else again. It was Chief Engineer Dr. Fritz Nallinger's pet project on which he labored long and hard to create the most technically sophisticated luxury car of its time. The concept of a prestige touring car of advanced engineering has traditionally been an important part of the Mercedes-Benz line, and the appearance of the first 300s at

Frankfurt was a tangible guarantee that Mercedes-Benz was back in business in the grand manner. The 300 represented a distillation of the Daimler-Benz expertise in sophisticated suspension via swing axles and coil springs. An interesting refinement was the electrical control of the auxiliary torsion bar rear suspension from the driver's seat, which permitted a fairly wide range of control over the rear suspension according to the weight being carried. Other chassis refinements included improved steering, hypoid bevel final drive, and dynamically balanced wheels.

The 300 sedan weighed 4210 pounds and was executed with traditionally Teutonic robustness. So it required rather some nerve to power such an automobile with an engine displacing only three litres. However, Mercedes-Benz once fielded a three litre racing car of 480 HP, and the 300 engine, while not quite that sophisticated, was anything but conventional. Designated the M186, the three litre engine used staggered valve placement and the head was built without openings, the spark plugs being fitted through the side of the block. The head and block were cut at corresponding thirty-degree angles as were the pistons. Notches were cut into the pistons which formed part of the very unusual combustion chamber.

The 300 was convincing evidence that Mercedes-Benz was still putting creative engineering ahead of all else. A comparison with the 5.4 litre 540K offers some interesting revelations. With only a little more than half the displacement, the unsupercharged 300 sedan put out 125 HP against the 540K's 115 in unsupercharged form. And apparently it even made those horses work harder because the conservative 300 sedan would out-accelerate a 540K sports roadster driven for maximum acceleration with the blower going. Factory specifications credited the 540K roadster (the lightest of the series) with 65 MPH in nineteen seconds; the

300 D hardtop limousine offered spaciousness, performance, and a Sybaritic sense of luxury. (*Courtesy, Daimler-Benz*)

The 300 series represented the height of technical sophistication in a luxurious touring car. Author's 300 C has low pivot single joint swing/axle, electrically operated auxiliary torsion bar suspension, and offers a satisfyingly secure and comfortable ride. Engine development showed a remarkable advance on this car; with 3 litres pulling 4210 pounds the performance *exceeded* the 5.4 litre 540 K of 1939. (*Photograph by the author*)

1951 300 was good for 60 MPH in under fifteen seconds. Top speeds of the two cars were virtually identical. While the 300 does not meet the preferences of prep school mentality with neck snapping acceleration so dearly loved by Americans, the author has never found its power inadequate over thousands of miles and nearly a decade of driving one.

As the ultimate effort to re-establish the three-pointed star in the postwar market, the 300 sedans were showpieces of Mercedes craftsmanship which equalled, and in some aspects surpassed, pre-war standards. The coachwork subtly combined classic and contemporary lines and complemented rather than betrayed both schools. After four years, the 300A progressed to the B-type with increased compression and 136 HP and shortly to the C-type with automatic transmission. An elegant four-door touring cabriolet was also available, and both versions soon traveled in elite and diplomatic circles carrying kings, presidents, popes, and at least one genuine emperor.

The M186 engine even in its developed 300C form was obviously intended for livelier things than trundling diplomats and debutants about in glistening black-lacquered limousines. One of those livelier things, the 300S Grand Touring Mercedes-Benz first appeared at the 1952 Salon de Paris and immediately captivated the crowds. The 300S was a worthy successor to the tradition of the 540K as a spirited but correct and thoroughly comfortable machine. Like the old "S" cars the 300S had charisma. It was the ultimate gentleman's carriage; fast and very roadable for sporting moods, elegant and soul satisfyingly luxurious for more hedonistic ones. Following the precedents of the 300 sedans the 300S Grand Touring was contemporary classic in styling, and the interior was a sumptuous little world of the best rolled and pleated leather tailored into wide, tranquilizing seats and accented with opulent slashes of polished wal-

The suave and elegant 300 soon found its way into diplomatic use. Here, President John F. Kennedy waves from the Mexican Presidential car, a fuel injected 300 D landau limousine. Car is black with beige leather interior. (*Courtesy, Daimler-Benz*)

nut. Enormous amounts of talented hand work was lavished on the 300S (about a thousand man hours per car) and the car was undeniably the end of an age of grace.

The 300S Mercedes-Benz was built on order only to a particular client's preferences and those preferences flowed in from a clientele like the Shah of Iran, the Aga Khan, the King of Jordan, the Prime Minister of Thailand, Sultan Mohamed Ben u. Mulai Arafa of Morocco (whose ancestor bought the very first royal car from Gottlieb Daimler in 1888), Lord Rosebury of England, Prince Alfonso of Hohenlohe, Gary Cooper, Bing Crosby, Mario Moreno, and Yvette Mimieux.

The 300S chassis was derived from the 300 sedans but was shortened from a 120-inch wheelbase to 114 inches, and the electrically controlled rear torsion bar auxiliary suspension was dropped in the interests of weight saving. The versatile M186 engine was revised once again, this time with a 7.8 to 1 compression ratio and three downdraft carburetors to give 150 HP and speed of over 110 MPH. In 1956 the 300Sc was introduced which used the same direct fuel injection engine as the 300SL sports car and raised the power output to over 200 HP. During its 1952–1957 production span, the 300S was created in three moods, the cabriolet landau, a roadster with disappearing top, and the fixed head coupe. In all, 760 were built, according to the following schedule:

| 300S | | 300Sc | |
|---|---|---|---|
| Cabriolet landau . . . 203 | | Cabriolet landau . . . . 49 | |
| Roadster . . . . . . 141 | | Roadster . . . . . . 53 | |
| Fixed head coupe . . 216 | | Fixed head coupe . . . 98 | |

In its 1954 models, Daimler-Benz re-styled the lower and middle range cars, the 180 and 220, and made some significant chassis improvements. For the first time since Hans

The 220a cabriolet appeared like a scaled down 300 S in styling, and was an elegant and comfortable car. (*Photograph by the author*)

The 220 S/SE convertible was an eminently civilized motorcar with svelte but classically subtle lines finished with a magnificent hand crafted interior of sumptuous leathercraft and graceful walnut wainscoting. (*Courtesy, Daimler-Benz*)

The 220 S cabriolet served as successor to the 300 S. It offered 120 HP, over 100 MPH top speed, and superb riding qualities. (*Courtesy, Daimler-Benz*)

View of the 300 D specially built for the Vatican. Precedents for the later "Grand 600" can be seen in the sumptuous rear compartment. (*Courtesy, Daimler-Benz*)

Nibel designed it in the early 1930s, his very successful dual joint swing axle was re-designed and now appeared as a low-pivot, single-joint swing axle. Besides permitting more room inside the car, Daimler-Benz reported that the new design offered "marked advantages in improved cornering, general refinement, and safety." The swing axle improvement was, of course, also adapted to the 300 series.

The new 220 of 1954 was a good car to own. It is difficult to say whether it was a practical luxury car or a luxurious practical car, for it contained equal measures of both qualities. Mechanically, it was straightforward, untemperamental, and economical to operate. Yet the subdued, modern coach-

The 300 Mercedes-Benz soon gained acceptance in elite and diplomatic circles. Here, Pope John XXIII rides through Rome in his specially built 300. (*Courtesy, Daimler-Benz*)

work was finished with meticulous attention to detail and a fine leather and walnut interior. The 220 proved to be a sturdy and durable car and even in America, where most drivers are not noted for being solicitous about the welfare of their automobiles, there are still many of these "demivintage" 220s in daily use. Later, the series was expanded with the dual carbureted 220S and the fuel injected 220SE.

A very attractive convertible version of the 220S was developed as a successor to the old 220 cabriolet, which had appeared basically as a "miniature 300S". In fact, the new

220 S/SE convertible was itself the replacement for the discontinued 300S. It was a svelte, modern automobile, yet classically subtle and in superb taste in any situation. It was an eminently civilized motorcar, finished with a magnificent hand worked interior of sumptuous leathercraft and some of the most graceful woodwork ever put into a car.

These models, with the 190SL sports roadster and the fuel injected 300D of 1958, carried Mercedes-Benz to the end of the 1950s and into a "new generation" of cars.

Chapter 9

# Return to the Circuits

The 300S Mercedes-Benz admirably met Enzo Ferrari's definition of a Grand Touring car as one "which incorporates the experience of racing in order to render daily use more enjoyable and secure." The 300S, of course, embodied many of the lessons learned in Mercedes's successful sweep of Grand Prix racing in the 1930s. But in a sense it went one step further than Ferrari's definition when the 300S itself became the basis from which one of the world's great sports machines was developed.

For the first time in twenty years there was a new Mercedes-Benz sports car on the road in 1952. In the next two years the *avant garde* 300SL won virtually every competition in sight while the world looked on with wonderment. And with considerable envy, for the 300SL was not released for public sale until the blitzkrieg of the circuits was nearly over.

In the early fifties, the job of developing a radically new Mercedes-Benz sports car was entrusted to the capable hands of Rudolf Uhlenhaut and his embryo racing depart-

Mercedes-Benz 300 S Grand Touring cabriolet was the ultimate gentleman's carriage; fast and roadable for sporting moods, and sumptuously luxurious and stylish for more hedonistic ones. (*Courtesy, Daimler-Benz*)

Fixed head coupe or "hardtop" version of the 300 S. In the original 300 S form the car was fitted with three downdraft carburetors and developed 150 HP. In the later 300 Sc version the 300 SL fuel injected sports car engine was fitted and horsepower rose to over 200 HP. (*Courtesy, Daimler-Benz*)

ment. Uhlenhaut was satisfied that the basic M186 three litre engine could be developed to provide the power, but the chassis was another problem entirely. The massive X-shaped oval tube frame used on the touring cars was prohibitively heavy and even the lightened 300S chassis was not a suitable prototype. Something entirely unconventional was called for, and Uhlenhaut's answer was characteristically efficient and ingenious. He replaced the concept of the ordinary chassis frame by a light, stiff structure made in a lattice pattern of thin welded steel tubing. The design assured that none of the members would have to endure a bending stress, the stresses running lengthwise only. The thin outer skin could be very light, since the lattice structure and not the body would carry all the stresses.

There was just one minor flaw in this arrangement which bothered everyone except the spectators who saw the fin-

The 300 S roadster built with a top which folded completely into the coachwork; 141 such 300 S roadsters were built. (*Courtesy, Daimler-Benz*)

ished cars on the track. This was the fact that because of the peculiar frame design and the scant fifty inches from road to roof, conventional front hinged doors could not be fitted and so the famous "gull wing" design with the doors hinged in the roof and opening upward was decided upon. To Daimler-Benz, especially team manager Alfred Neubauer, this innovation represented something of an uncertain compromise; but to sports car fans it was totally unrestrained glamour. In the production model of the 300SL gull wing coupe, 1954–1956, access to the austere passenger compartment *is* on the awkward side, although the inconvenience is more than offset by watching the entry and exit of your miniskirted passenger.

The development of the 300SL engine presents some interesting lessons in just what extremes can be reached in perfecting a basically modest but flexible engine. Originally,

The 300 series sedans represented the ultimate effort to re-establish Mercedes-Benz in the postwar luxury market, and were showpieces of craftsmanship which equaled or surpassed prewar standards. (*Photograph by the author*)

Luxurious leather and walnut interior of the hardtop 300 D fuel-injected 180 HP sedan, current 1958–1963. (*Courtesy, Daimler-Benz*)

the M186 300 engine produced 125 HP which was increased to 136 HP in the 300C and 150 HP to 200 HP in the 300S/Sc. In the very earliest specimens of the 300SL, three downdraft carburetors were fitted, yielding 200 HP (at least one of these early cars was also supercharged) but as soon as the direct fuel injection system was perfected and installed the horsepower output rose to 240 (SAE) and the car could accelerate smoothly on top gear from 15 MPH to its top speed of 166 MPH. This was about double the power extracted from the original three litre engine, and the 300SL power unit was now officially designated the M198.

Now, all that remained was a means of mounting the rather tall engine in a car that hugged so close to the road. The solution was to mount the engine diagonally, as it was

A modern classic, the 300 SL "gull wing" coupe. The tubular lattice chassis on the car—which stood only 50 inches high—obviated the use of conventional front hinged doors. Daimler-Benz was never enthralled with the idea, considering it a compromise. Spectators and buyers found it glamorous. (*Courtesy, Daimler-Benz*)

King Hussein of Jordan maintained a stable of Mercedes-Benz cars for desert racing. Here, he drives his 300 SL gull wing coupe, carrying an interesting license plate. (*Courtesy, Daimler-Benz*)

done on the 1938 W163. The 300SL was canted forty degrees to the left and a suitable new oil pan and manifolds were fitted. This oblique mounting allowed the very low silhouette to be carried out successfully and permitted the driver and passenger an extraordinary view of the road.

The application of direct fuel injection to the 300SL Mercedes-Benz was an intriguing example of history repeating itself almost verbatim. In the First World War aero engine, starvation at high altitudes prompted the development of supercharging. After the war, the technique was adapted to a series of championship sports cars. In the Second World War Daimler-Benz perfected fuel injection for even higher-flying aircraft engines and again adapted the process, postwar, to a classic, champion sports car.

While fuel injection is hardly a simple process, it can be explained fairly easily. Succinctly, the *einspritzer* is the most efficient way of feeding fuel to the engine yet devised, displacing the carburetor entirely. The fuel is pumped from the gas line to a set of injection nozzles, one at each intake valve. Before the fuel is injected into each cylinder for combustion it has been "metered" or measured very carefully according to the exact needs of the engine at that moment to assure that the mixture is never too rich or too lean. The chief values of fuel injection are, first, complete combustion and maximum efficiency from the engine and, second, the fact that at equal power output a fuel injected engine will use less gasoline than the same engine with carburetors. Because of their more complete combustion, fuel injected engines also tend to exhale fewer pollutants into the atmosphere. Fuel injection may be *direct* where the fuel is injected into each cylinder individually with a plunger for each cylinder, as in the 300SL, or via *port injection* in which fewer plungers may be used and the fuel is injected into a manifold and then into the cylinder.

Armed with the 300SL, the Mercedes-Benz Racing Team appeared on a racing circuit in May of 1952 with a new car for the first time in thirteen years. The amazing thing was not so much that they were there, or even that they had chosen perhaps the most difficult course in the history of motor racing, the Mille Miglia, but that Alfred Neubauer's racing team had emerged in a perfect state of preservation with all the old time fanatical efficiency intact. Three 300SLs, driven by Karl Kling, Herman Lang, and Rudolf Caracciola were entered against a well entrenched field of Ferraris whose native drivers knew the course through the Italian countryside as well as they knew the words to Santa

Lucia. Despite the fact that the Germans could know only the basics of the course (although Caracciola had won the Mille Miglia twenty one years before) and lost one of their cars when Karl Kling hit a mile post only about a tenth of the way through the race, they put on an astonishing show and took second and fourth places.

Throughout the rest of their maiden season, the 300SLs racked up a victory in the German Grand Prix at Nurburgring, a 1–2 win in the rugged Carrera Pan-Americana road race in Mexico (with an amazing 103 MPH *average*), and a "Mercedes trademark" 1–2–3 victory at the Grand Prix of Bern. But the greatest plum of all came in mid-June in France—the first and only Mercedes-Benz victory ever at the super-celebrated "Twenty Four Hours of Le Mans". And it was a 1–2 win at that. If anyone in the racing fraternity still had any doubts about Mercedes-Benz, the signal victory at Sarthe effectively dissolved them. The three-pointed star had indeed returned to the circuits.

With the 300SL established as the obvious and worthy descendant of the triumphant SSK of the twenties, Mercedes-Benz now moved on to re-create its domination of the Grand Prix circuits. As soon as the Formula I Grand Prix formula was announced for 1954–1957 (2.5 litres for unsupercharged engines, 0.75 litre for supercharged engines) Uhlenhaut's Racing Department set to work on a new racing machine with all the old enthusiasm that it had lavished on the W125.

In building the new 2.5 litre Grand Prix car, Uhlenhaut borrowed heavily from the 300SL, using the lattice type tubular frame and the low-pivot, single-joint swing axle. To this he added the innovation of completely inboard brakes to reduce unsprung weight, with the front drums running very close to each other directly in front of the engine in a space not much wider than the engine itself. The

Because of the W 196's sustained high revolutions, ordinary valve operation was inadequate and replaced by Dr. Fritz Nallinger's "desmodromic valve gear." (*Courtesy, Daimler-Benz*)

rear drums ran directly behind the driver's seat, and the very adequately sized drums were turbo cooled, receiving fresh air from scoops built into the coachwork. Torsion bars were fitted to all four wheels.

The W196 engine was a radical departure even for Mercedes-Benz. Direct fuel injection was of course *de rigeur* on the 2.5 litre double overhead-cam, in-line eight, but because of the engine's sustained high revolutions ordinary valve operation was deemed inadequate. As a more efficient replacement, the "desmodromic valve gear" was devised by Chief Engineer Dr. Fritz Nallinger who described it as, "A mechanical forced timing device for opening and closing the valves quickly by a guided motion." Mated to a five-speed box, the very complex engine (actually two four cylinder units with power taken from the center of the crankshaft) was mounted in the chassis at a thirty degree angle to accommodate the low, aerodynamic coachwork. The W196 easily yielded 300 HP, and with almost British understatement Daimler-Benz said that "the acceleration and elasticity of this engine were quite unique, and there always remained a little power in reserve."

The innovations of the W196 were not confined to the engine and chassis; they extended all the way out to its silver skin. Recalling the daring aerodynamic record cars of 1938, Uhlenhaut invested a lot of time in wind tunnel testing to develop a body for the W196 that was both functionally sound and strikingly elegant. It was a novelty to see a full Grand Prix car appear with its wheels neatly sheathed in svelte, streamlined fenders, and the result was very pleasing to the eye. Unfortunately, it was not so pleasing to the eyes of the team drivers who were accustomed to see those naked wheels up there in front of them. And when it came to things that might win or lose races, Mercedes-Benz drivers—with Alfred Neubauer to back them up—were accustomed to getting what they wanted. Once, when Stirling Moss became disenchanted with the gearbox in his car and suggested some changes a new one was designed to his specifications, built, and running within twenty-four hours. So, as an alternate to the streamlined car, a more normal open wheel monoposto version of the W196 appeared later in the 1954 season.

In our affluent "super society" the word "fabulous" is bandied about with rather reckless abandon, describing everything from milady's newest paper panties to Friday night's feature at the drive-in. However, as applied to the W196's racing record, fabulous is merely an adequate description. Mercedes-Benz raced in Grand Prix competition for the 1954 and 1955 seasons. In that time they delivered a blistering broadside to Enzo Ferrari's dominating red cars. The team seemed to be under the definite impression that there was no such thing as a fifteen-year gap since the last Mercedes-Benz Grand Prix car had put rubber to road on the elite European circuits.* The W196 was entered for fifteen Grand Prix races during its tenure and won twelve of them, with seven double victories, one triple victory, and one quadruple victory. In 1954, Mercedes-Benz took the Grand Prix events of France, Germany, Switzerland, Italy, and Spain, as well as the Avus Races. In 1955, they took the Grand Prix honors of Argentina, Buenos Aires, Belgium, Holland, Britain, and Italy. As a member of the victorious Mercedes-Benz team, the talented Argentinian driver, Juan Manuel Fangio, won the world's championship by seventeen points. Satisfied that the traditional superiority on the

---

* Pre-war three litre cars ran in the Peron Cup and the Eva Peron Grand Prix in February of 1951, taking second and third places in both races. Neubauer regarded the Argentinian adventure as a dry run for what was to come.

circuits was still on tap, Mercedes-Benz retired from Grand Prix racing at the end of 1955 and turned its energies to other things.

Concurrent with the 1954–1955 Grand Prix effort, Mercedes-Benz continued in sports car racing, but with a car quite different from the original 300SL. The double overhead-cam, eight-cylinder, fuel-injected straight-eight, 2.5 litre W196 engine was stroked to 78 mm (equal to the bore) to yield a three litre displacement. This revised engine was then laid at a thirty degree angle into a tubular lattice chassis virtually identical to the W196 (including the inboard brakes), and fitted with stunning aerodynamic sports coachwork similar to that on the streamlined W196. The resulting machine was, in effect, a "sporterized" W196, and in fact was known at the Stuttgart works as the W196S (Sports). However, the 300SL had just gone into general production and publicity executives saw a chance to tie the two cars together in the public mind by calling the new super sports car (which was never offered for public sale) the 300SLR (Sports, leicht, Rennwagen). Despite one awful, cataclysmic piece of bad luck which would befall it, the 300SLR would retire at the end of 1955 as the most successful sports car in the history of racing.

Toward the end of the 1954 season, Alfred Neubauer invited the great English driver Stirling Moss to become a member of the Mercedes-Benz Racing Team. Coincidentally, or otherwise, this was just the time that the first prototype 300SLR had been completed and was being tested. Moss, Juan Fangio, Karl Kling, and Hans Hermann were to make an epic assault on that most challenging of races, the Mille Miglia. Karl Kling's 300SL had taken second place in 1952, but nothing less than a repeat of Rudolf Caracciola's masterful 1931 win in his SSK would do. Neubauer, of course, bit into the job with his characteristically

The redoubtable rennleiter, Alfred Neubauer; the most famous—and successful—team manager in the history of motor racing.

precise perseverance. There were two practice 300SLRs available to him; and four fresh ones were being readied for the real thing.

The practice cars were first run at Monza, Uhlenhaut himself doing some of the breaking-in and turning in stiff lap times that were fractionally faster than those of the full Grand Prix car. Although it is not generally known, Uhlenhaut is a first class race driver and could have ranked with

When Mercedes-Benz team drivers became disturbed over not being able to see the front wheels of the streamlined W 196 a more normal open wheel monoposto version was made up. Engine was mounted at a thirty degree angle to achieve the low silhouette. (*Courtesy, Daimler-Benz*)

the aces had he not chosen to build cars rather than drive them. The year before, he had been similarly practicing with W196s at Nurburgring and had become distressed over some of Juan Manuel Fangio's lap times. Climbing into the car himself, he proceeded to knock nearly five seconds off the time recorded by the world's champion driver.

More practice, while Neubauer drilled his troops with Prussian precision through thousands of miles. Then, on to Italy where the course itself could be studied over and over. Neubauer believed that innovation was no substitute for preparation. He insisted that his drivers know how to service the 300SLR even down to the complex fuel injection system. This proved not to be wasted effort for Juan Fangio indeed had to stop and replace a fuel injection pipe.

Still, it was not enough; as always, the odds seemed with the native Italians until Moss's co-pilot, British motoring writer Denis Jenkinson, came up with an inspired idea. Together, Moss and Jenkinson had assembled detailed notes on the one thousand miles of Italy, but it was rather difficult to leaf through a notebook in an open car at 170 MPH. It was Jenkinson's idea to transcribe the details onto a seventeen foot roll of paper which could be read through a plexiglass window in a box as he cranked the reel of paper. As Jenkinson "read the road" from his lap he relayed the details to Moss via thirteen hand signals. The Italians undoubtedly regarded this as the worst sort of Anglo-Teutonic skullduggery, but there were no rules against "programming" the course on a home-made computer.

In the Mille Miglia, the cars were numbered according to their departure times and Moss and Jenkinson's car, scheduled to leave Brescia at 7:22 AM on the first of May, was marked "722". As it stood on the starting ramp in the Italian morning sun surrounded by officials and spectators and the starter with his flag in hand, the silver car stood as the

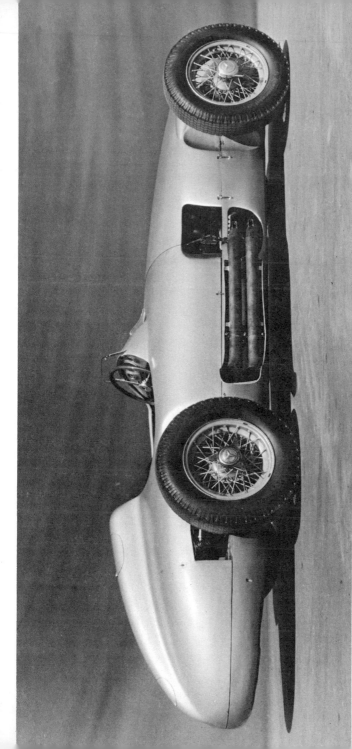

The W 196 2.5 litre Formula I car represented a very sophisticated approach to Grand Prix racing in 1954–1955. Its engine was a double overhead-camshaft, in-line eight which substituted a "desmodromic valve gear" for conventional valve operation. The brake drums were completely inboard to reduce unsprung weight. (*Courtesy, Daimler-Benz*)

Rudolf Uhlenhaut invested time in wind tunnel tests to develop a streamlined body for the W 196 Grand Prix car that was both functionally sound and strikingly elegant. The W 196 is certainly one of the prettiest Grand Prix cars ever built. (*Courtesy, Daimler-Benz*)

culmination of the work of hundreds of people. And none of them had worked harder than Rudolf Uhlenhaut. Back in his office at Stuttgart, a large chart hung on the wall listing the races entered for 1955, the cars, their drivers, and empty spaces for results. In about ten hours that blank space beside "Mille Miglia" would be filled, or not. Curiously, number 722 seemed almost a personification of Rudolf Uhlenhaut's own German-English mixture; a purely German car piloted by Englishmen and running with a British-born plan. Somehow the red, white, and blue Union Jacks painted on the head fairings behind Moss's and Jenkinson's helmets did not seem at all out of place.

When Moss rolled down the ramp at twenty-two minutes past seven o'clock, Fangio, Kling, and Hermann in the other 300SLRs and most of the 499 other contestants had preceded him. The earlier stages of the race, across to Verona, Vicenza, and Padua and down the Adriatic Coast through Rimini and to Pescara offered opportunities for flat out driving along the straight stretches. Moss accelerated to near the car's 180 MPH plus top speed and relied on Jenkinson to relay road conditions ahead. All went well until they hit a dip in the road that wasn't on Jenkinson's scroll and at the crest the Mercedes took off and flew about two hundred feet through the air. Moss held the wheel motionless and waited the eternity that it took to land. The 300SLR was an extraordinarily rugged car which could shrug off all but the most serious race-inflicted injuries and this time it came down like a big bird and roared off toward Rome as if nothing had happened.

At Rome, number 722 was in the premier position, so now in addition to the swarm of Ferraris and Maseratis et al Moss had to fight the unfailing tradition that "He who leads at Rome never leads at Brescia." The way back to Brescia led through the mountain country and here Jenkinson's

As 300 SLR number 722 stood on the starting ramp in the Italian morning sun about to start in the XXII Mille Miglia it represented the work and hopes of hundreds of people. (*Courtesy, Daimler-Benz*)

road reader came into its own, permitting Moss to take blind hills and curves at 175 MPH and *know* what was on the other side without resorting to a stressed memory. In this mountain stretch number 722 was seen to pull away and *pass* an observation plane that had been filming it.

A flying stone through the gas tank had meanwhile accounted for Hermann's 300SLR and a crowd of excited Italians waiting in the middle of the road for a glimpse of the cars had forced Karl Kling off into a ditch near Rimini. It was now up to Moss and Fangio, who both drove like inspired demons in the home stretch. Moss made the round trip—driving single handedly—in ten hours, seven minutes, and forty eight seconds at an average speed of 97.90 MPH (the all-time record), and Fangio came in thirty-two minutes later to make it a 1–2 Mercedes victory. It was a classic feat of endurance, for both car and driver. The 300SLR never had its hood raised during the full thousand miles, receiving only gasoline (at re-fueling stations which Neubauer himself had set up) and a change of the rear tires. Denis Jenkinson records that after the race number 722 was sent back to the factory for testing and produced the same power curve that it had before the race.

Mercedes had re-affirmed Caracciola's 1931 Mille Miglia victory and now it set out to duplicate Lang's 1952 mastery of Le Mans, this time with the 300SLR. It has always been

Stirling Moss's co-pilot in the 1955 Mille Miglia, British motoring writer Denis Jenkinson, transcribed the details of the 1000-mile course onto a 17-foot scroll which he unreeled and relayed to Moss by hand signals. The technique permitted Moss to take blind hills at 175 MPH and know what was on the other side without relying on a stressed memory. (*Courtesy, Daimler-Benz*)

Off and running. Moss and Jenkinson blaze away from Brescia with a thousand miles of Italy before them. Moss broke the tradition that "He who leads at Rome never leads at Brescia." (*Courtesy, Daimler-Benz*)

A 300 SLR, battered in the 1955 Targa Florio, gets attention from the incredibly efficient Mercedes-Benz pit crew. The 300 SLR was an amazingly robust car and could shrug off all but the most serious race-inflicted injuries. (*Courtesy, Daimler-Benz*)

Mercedes strategy to tailor its cars to specific courses where possible, and so a special 300SLR was evolved to meet the Le Mans challenge.

First, since only one man would be in the car at a time, the passenger compartment was covered with an aluminum "lid" and the streamlined head fairing was used only behind the driver's seat. This head fairing normally contained the tank fill (see photo of Moss's Targa Florio car being fueled) but on the special Le Mans cars the tank fill was placed behind the head fairing. The reason for this was so that a hydraulically operated air brake could be raised and lowered to assist in braking. (See photo of car number 19 with air brake in raised position.) Along the fast Mulsanne straight the 300SLR would reach speeds of 180 MPH and just after that would encounter a nearly ninety degree curve requiring downshifting to second gear. Naturally, this put a tremendous strain on the car and the air brake was devised to assist the drum brakes. As the driver approached the sharp Mulsanne curve the plan was for him to pull a lever which activated the air brake panel and snapped it up into the rushing air stream. There was a mechanism fitted to the gearbox which, when the driver downshifted into second gear, automatically lowered the air brake panel without further attention from the driver. In addition to the braking assist, the panel also tended to steady the car on the road and was helpful in taking corners at high speed.

Three 300 SLRs were entered for Le Mans with teams consisting of Fangio and Moss, Kling and Simon, and Levegh and Fitch. The race started with all the traditional carnival and camping-out gaiety and the dash of the "Le Mans start". Then about two and a half hours into the race Pierre Levegh tangled with a little Austin-Healy near the pit area, and what might have been a minor incident suddenly turned into the worst racing disaster since the Paris-

Mercedes strategy is to tailor cars to specific courses and this specialized 300 SLR was evolved for Le Mans. The tank fill was moved back to allow for a hydraulically operated air brake which was intended to assist the brakes in a sharp curve just after the 180 MPH Mulsanne straight. (*Courtesy, Daimler-Benz*)

Fangio, Moss and Kling at a curve in the 1955 International Eifel Race. Mercedes-Benz team finished first, second, and fourth. (*Courtesy, Daimler-Benz*)

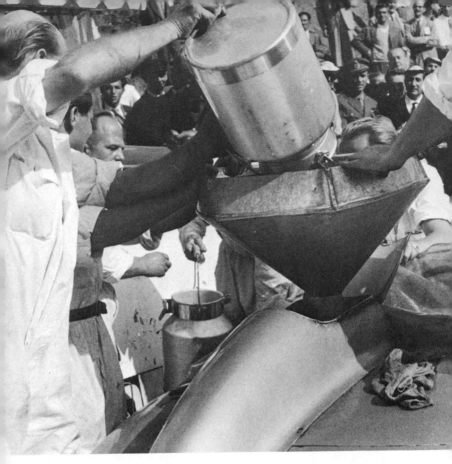

Moss-Collins car being fueled in the 1955 Targa Florio. Note the tank fill concealed in the head fairing. Moss-Collins won the race, with Fangio-Kling second, and Titterington-Fitch fourth. (*Courtesy, Daimler-Benz*)

Madrid over half a century before. The front end of Levegh's car number 0006/55 careened out of a cloud of dust and into a tightly packed knot of spectators, killing over eighty people and injuring many more. Horrified, Neubauer got on the telephone to Stuttgart and an emergency meeting of the board of directors was called. Although no fault could be traced to Mercedes-Benz cars or

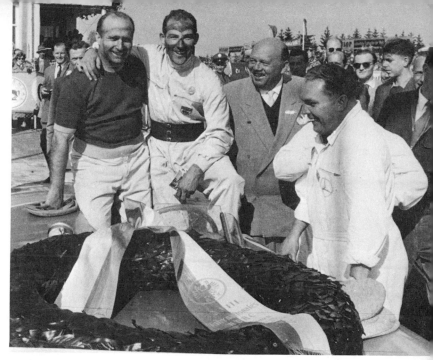

Juan Manuel Fangio and Stirling Moss, World's Champion race drivers, after the 1955 International Eifel Race. (*Courtesy, Daimler-Benz*)

drivers, they decided to withdraw the two remaining 300 SLRs from the race as a mark of respect. At 2:00 AM Sunday morning Alfred Neubauer stood in front of the Mercedes-Benz pits and with a black flag brought his cars in. At that time the Fangio-Moss car dominated the race with a two lap lead. A Jaguar was second with the Kling-Simon 300SLR hot on its heels.

The public reaction to the 1955 Le Mans was much the same as it had been to the Paris-Madrid, and both the French and Germans cancelled their Grand Prix events. It would have been a sad thing for Mercedes-Benz to have concluded its great postwar racing epoch on such a tragic note, and so it was decided to participate as planned in the rest of the year's events for which the 300SLR or W196 had been entered. The Grand Prix cars returned victories in the Dutch, British, and Italian Grand Prix races, and the 300 SLRs won the Swedish Grand Prix, the Irish Tourist Trophy, and concluded both the season and their career with a spectacular 1–2 win in the Targa Florio. Nothing, of course, could overshadow the horror of "the black Le Mans" that year, but it is worthwhile to recall that the 300SLR won every race in which it was ever entered except the 1955 Le Mans from which it was voluntarily withdrawn while still in the dominant position. The author knows of no other car in racing history that can make the same claim.

After 1955, Mercedes-Benz withdrew from organized racing, although it still entered stock cars in rallies and endurance runs where they continued to enhance the marque's reputation and add to its present total of over 4400 victories on road and track.

## A Summary of Mercedes-Benz Racing 1954–55

### 1954 Formula I racing (2.5 litres)

French Grand Prix—First, second
English Grand Prix—Fourth
German Grand Prix—First, fourth
Swiss Grand Prix—First, third
Italian Grand Prix—First, fourth
Avus Race—First, second, third
Spanish Grand Prix—Third

### 1955 Formula I racing (2.5 litres)

Argentinian Grand Prix—First, fourth
Belgium Grand Prix—First, second
Dutch Grand Prix—First, second
English Grand Prix—First, second, third, fourth
Italian Grand Prix—First, second

*1955 Non-Formula racing (2.5 litre chassis with 3 litre 300 SLR engine)*

Grand Prix of Buenos Aires—First, second, fourth

*1955 Sports Car Racing* (300 SLR, 3 litre)
XXII Mille Miglia—First, second
International Eifel Race—First, second, fourth
Swedish Grand Prix—First, second
Irish Tourist Trophy—First, second, third
Targa Florio—First, second, fourth.

In the 1954–55 seasons, Mercedes-Benz cars won the following World Championships:

1954: Racing Car World Championship (World Champion Juan Manuel Fangio)

1955: European Touring Car Championship (European Champion Werner Engel)

International Sports Car Championship (Marque World Championship—Coupe des Constructeurs, 300SLR)

Racing Car World Championship (World Champions: Juan Manuel Fangio, Stirling Moss)

American Sports Car Championship (Paul O'Shea, 300SL)

# Chapter 10

# Mercedes-Benz Today

With a decade of astonishing accomplishments, Mercedes-Benz put the 1950s among its proudest and most productive years. The company entered the 1950s with little more than the memory and remnants of an automotive empire, and with one small, basically pre-war, economy car. Throughout the next ten years Daimler-Benz produced an outstanding series of luxury cars impressive Grand Touring cars, dominated Grand Prix and sports car racing, perfected and mass-produced diesel cars, re-established its various non-automotive capacities, and entered the 1960s with the most technically advanced motorcars in the world.

When Mercedes-Benz retired from racing in 1955, it redirected that energy and expertise into the development of passenger cars. The following year, a new project aimed at a complete revision of the middle-range Mercedes, the 220, was begun. Extensive experiments were carried out with the 220S/SE on which the new low-pivot, single-joint swing-axle had been pioneered in 1954. If Mercedes-Benz racing car preparation was impressive it was nothing compared to what went into the development of the first "new generation" cars. Two million test miles, more millions of dollars, and three years later the new car was ready to debut at the 1959 International Automobile Exposition in Frankfort. Incidentally, Mercedes designers are expected to put themselves in the driver's seat long before any of their clients do, and so quite a few of those test miles, over some of the toughest roads in Europe, were racked up by Dr. Fritz Nallinger and Rudolf Uhlenhaut themselves. Even a "closed rally" from Stuttgart to Naples and back for the designer-engineers as well as for test drivers was part of the evaluation of the new design.

The powerplant of the new 220b for 1960 was left virtually unchanged, but extremely close attention was paid to suspension, roadability, and driving comfort. The proven low-pivot, single-joint swing-axle was modified by the addition of a third compensating coil spring mounted horizontally in the middle of the rear axle, a technique adopted from the 300SL to give greater stability in a fast curve. Shock absorbers were re-located closer to the wheels, and the independent front suspension was also re-designed with better handling and control in mind. The result of these integrated chassis improvements was a car which seemed comfortably soft sprung yet which still retained sports car stability. A lower and wider body of integral construction and squarish modern design was shown at the Frankfort show. The coachwork skillfully blended the traditional Mercedes-Benz radiator grille into the modern milieu, although the slightly tail-finned rear deck treatment was a disappointment. The frontal facade with the European style single large headlamp lens was rather more graceful and impressive than the vertically mounted dual sealed beam headlamps used on the American export models.

When a new car is developed at Stuttgart the tradition is

The "gull wing" 300 SL was the glamour sports machine of the 1950s. Here, "Skitch" Henderson, a Mercedes afficionado of long standing, talks about his 300 SL to a TV audience. (*Courtesy, Mr. Henderson*)

for it to be tempered in the fires of open competition. The Monte Carlo Rally is to touring cars just as brutal and rugged a challenge as the Mille Miglia or Targa Florio was to Mercedes racing cars. Much of the course runs through splendid mountain scenery in country offering perhaps the most rugged driving in the world. The Monte Carlo has been nicknamed "the roulette rally" because sudden storms, landslides, or washed-out roads can juggle contestants' chances with all the fickleness of a clicking roulette ball. Mercedes entered three teams of new 220SE's in the Monte Carlo, and prefaced the event with three full months of practice over the difficult mountain route under the direction of racing driver Karl Kling.

Starting points for the Monte Carlo stretched from Athens to Oslo, but whatever route a driver picked he was

Mercedes-Benz 300 SE Characteristics: Light-metal fuel injection engine, air suspension, automatic transmission, servo steering and disc brakes.

Instrumentation and dash panel of the 600 Mercedes. Tests proved that the fat-rimmed steering wheel design does not fatigue the driver's hands the way older thin rim designs do. (*Courtesy, Daimler-Benz*)

going to face a lot of European January in the mountains. The Mercedes-Benz team, led by Walter Schock, a Stuttgart food broker by occupation and professional driver by avocation, and Rudolf Moll chose to leave from Warsaw after a careful analysis of weather predictions. The route led through some of the most horrendous terrain imaginable, including totally ice-covered roads which laughed at steel studded snow tires. At one point, Schock and Moll noticed a competing car perched in a tree where it had landed after leaving the road. Fewer than half of the starters ever reached the sunshine of Monte Carlo at all.

Walter Schock and Rudolf Moll did make Monte Carlo, and, figuratively (with fewer penalty points) ahead of anyone else. And the other two 220SEs were right behind them to make it a "Mercedes trademark" 1–2–3 win. A plus, the frosting on the cake, was the Manufacturers' Team Prize. It was a resounding victory for Mercedes-Benz and one which —without detracting one millimeter from the drivers' skill and stamina—could very well not have been won without the superb suspension of the 220SEs. Mercedes went on that year to enter and win other touring car rallies from Greece to Norway and piled up enough victories to earn the European Championship for 1960.

The next year, with Europe safely in hand, Mercedes took on the Dark Continent in the grueling African Rally, an 8700-mile run through dust, desert and jungle from Algiers to Capetown. Here, there was precedent for the exotic

The interior of the 600 Mercedes limousine presents an oasis of opulence with rolled and pleated leather or velour mohair upholstery and glistening burled-walnut trim and cabinetry. Space is provided for radio, television, and telephone connections or a small bar. (*Courtesy, Daimler-Benz*)

The 600 Mercedes-Benz in sedan form has a 218-inch overall length, a top speed of 128 MPH, and acceleration of 0 to 50 MPH in seven seconds. A master hydraulic system latches the doors, adjusts the seats, opens and closes the windows and sliding roof, and even lifts the spare tire out of its compartment. (*Courtesy, Daimler-Benz*)

The world's finest automobile, the "Grand Mercedes" 600 limousine. A three-ton, 246-inch-long car, the 600 nevertheless has the speed, handling, and superb suspension of a top quality sports car. (*Courtesy, Daimler-Benz*)

challenge facing the four 220SEs which had been entered. In 1959, Karl Kling drove a 190D to victory in 170 hours over the whole horrible 8727 miles (including crossing the Sahara in a sandstorm) without so much as a single repair or tire change. Kling again piloted the lead 220SE in the 1961 African Rally, this time through 7200 miles of hazards ranging from freezing and 115-degree temperatures to a prairie fire. Putting his racing reflexes to work, Kling pushed the fuel-injected 2.2 litre for all it was worth, and at one point in the Sahara temporarily outdistanced a Daimler-Benz observation plane. He also outdistanced the competition, finishing first with other Mercedes-Benz cars in second and fifth position.

In 1961, Daimler-Benz celebrated seventy-five years of building automobiles, longer than any other manufacturer. Appropriately, Daimler's diamond jubilee year was sort of a moment frozen in time in which models representing Mercedes' past, present, and future were simultaneously in production. The catalogue ranged from the 180 economy sedan, really an updated 170 tracing its lineage back to the early 1930s—to the 300 D luxury sedan and 300 SL sports roadster, the pride of the 1950s—and on to the 220 SE and 300 SE, the first of the "new generation" Mercedes and clearly the shape of things to come. The jubilee year was marked with the introduction of the 220SE coupe and convertible models which blended the sophistication of the 220SE suspension and power units into a subtle synthesis of a sports-touring car with front disc brakes. In the same year, the concept was expanded to the 300SE coupe/convertible with self adjusting air suspension, Daimler-Benz's own shifting automatic gear transmission, disc brakes all around, and servo steering.

Daimler's celebrated its seventy-fifth anniversary with the opening of the new Daimler-Benz Museum, a three-story

38,000-square-foot building housing over one hundred exhibits dating back to the first Daimler and Benz engines of 1885–86. The great Daimler-Benz collection, begun in the days of Gottlieb Daimler, Karl Benz and Wilhelm Maybach, had grown through the years and was then largely destroyed and dispersed in World War II. Nevertheless, Daimler-Benz recovered, restored, and collected whatever it could, including a Mercedes "Sixty" with touring limousine coachwork used by the original Mercedes customer, Emil Jellinek. The effort paid off as one of the world's great automotive museums, and one where some of the exhibits can be wheeled off the floor, fueled up, and still beat almost anything on the road.

A significant ingredient of the "new generation" Mercedes cars is the heavy emphasis on safety as an integral part of the concept, design, and construction of the car. Safety was, incidentally, a factor on Stuttgart drawing boards long before American legislation made it mandatory and "fashionable". Uhlenhaut and his engineers started with the obvious premise that the basis of a safe car is its ability to *avoid* accidents. First, the driver should be able to see as well as possible, so he sits higher in a Mercedes than in most other cars and does not peer through the steering wheel. On the current 250 and 280 and 300 sedans the glass area extends nearly into the roof (without loss of structural rigidity) and from the inside the "pagoda" hardtop the 280SL gives very nearly the impression of being an open car.

Secondly, to ward off fatigue the driver should be as comfortable as possible. Daimler's orthopedic physicians ran tests to devise the best kind of seats and found that genuine comfort does not come from a plushy soft seat, but rather from a correctly contoured firm seat to alleviate muscle cramp and fatigue and maintain normal blood circulation. Since a driver generally spends more time behind the wheel

The "new generation" Mercedes-Benz philosophy with respect to sports cars has evolved the 280 SL, a strikingly individualistic and contemporary car that combines Grand Touring luxury with the lively qualities of a small sports car. (*Courtesy, Daimler-Benz*)

than in his fireside easy chair his car seat *should* be better engineered. The physicians' tests showed that their scientifically designed firm seats effectively fought driver fatigue and maintained alertness on long drives. Also to fight driver fatigue, special efforts were made to damp out semi-hypnotic noises and vibrations and tests proved that the odd-looking and often maligned fat-rimmed Mercedes steering wheel fatigued the driver's hands much less over long periods than the old thin rimmed wheels.

In avoiding trouble, a driver's first line of defense consists of his suspension, steering, and brakes. As we have seen, the severe emphasis on suspension in the development of the new 220s in 1960 produced a car which combined a safe and stable ride with civilized softness. While the usual Detroit-style soft suspension provides a luxurious ride at low and medium speeds it can become dangerously unstable at high speed or on uneven road surfaces. Daimler's experiments offered a way to the best of both worlds—sports-type suspension for safety, touring type for comfort. Mercedes engineers approached steering with a similar intent—to marry the natural "road telegraphing" feel of manual steering to power steering without the ordinary "blurring" effect which other power steering units tend to produce and which seem to isolate the driver from his car. Mercedes-Benz has been especially successful at this. When *Road and Track* magazine tested the power-steered 230SL one of the test drivers wasn't even aware that the car *had* power steering, which is the very highest compliment he could have paid it!

Mercedes-Benz braking efficiency and reliability are among the best in the world. Four-wheel, power-assisted disc brakes and dual circuit brake lines are standard equipment on all models from the least expensive on up to the 600 limousine. As an example of Mercedes philosophy that engineering should be better than it has to be, each of the disc brakes on the front wheels of the 600 is capable of dissipating 450 horsepower! In a panic stop from 80 MPH, the 600 will come to rest in 4.7 seconds, quicker than any other luxury car in the world.

In spite of all precautions, such as increasing a driver's efficiency, thus reducing his chance for error, and providing him with the best suspension, steering, and brakes, accidents still happen. In that case, the driver's next line of defense for survival is to have a car designed to shield him from the impact produced by a collision. Contrary to popular belief, a large, heavy, tanklike car does not necessarily offer the best, or even adequate, protection in an accident. Beginning with the "new generation" 220 of 1960 Mercedes began building the central passenger compartment of its cars from a unit structure of welded steel that is extremely rigid. However, the front and rear section of the car were designed to *collapse* progressively under impact in order to *absorb* most of the shock of a collision and prevent it from being transmitted to the passenger compartment. In effect, the front and rear of a Mercedes are great shock absorbers between the passengers and road hazards.

Tremendous deceleration force is produced when a moving car hits an object and stops almost instantly. Tests have shown that a human being can safely withstand a force equal to about sixty times the pull of gravity in such a situation, but of course the "G" force can rise to many times this in a serious accident. In a series of tests with the collapsible front and rear sections, a force of well over 800 times the pull of gravity was recorded at the front bumper at the instant of impact. By the time this force reached the firewall the energy absorbing design had reduced it to 480 Gs, and by the time the force of the collision reached the driver's seat it was well under the permissible 60 Gs.

In a front end collision one of the greatest dangers to a driver is not only being thrown forward onto the steering wheel and column, but also having it thrust up at him like a spear by the frontal impact to the steering system, even if he is held in place by his seat belt. In many cars where the steering box is placed ahead of the wheel axis, it is virtually impossible to prevent the steering column from being pushed back into the driver's chest in a head-on crash. However, in Mercedes design the steering box is mounted *behind* the wheel axis and is further shielded by a recess in the frame. In the event of a front end crash the impact is transferred to the chassis and cannot thrust the steering column into the passenger compartment. Further, there is a telescopic "energy absorbing impact damper" mounted between the steering wheel and the end of the steering column (which ends just beyond the firewall) which is designed to "give" on impact from both directions. This offers protection against either a frontal impact or in case the driver is thrown forward onto the padded steering wheel.

Other accident contingencies are protected against by padded instrument panels which also yield on impact, recessed door handles, spring mounted rear view mirrors which release under sixteen pounds tension, a windshield which pops out on impact, and control knobs and switches made of soft, flexible material. Mercedes doors stay shut during an accident and will still open afterward thanks to what are probably the best and most foolproof "safety-cone" door locks ever put on a car. If they are ever really needed even the $23.00 that it costs the company to make and install each one seems cheap.

Today Mercedes-Benz offers the most genuinely diversified line of automobiles in the world, running from the serious and durable economy of the 220 Diesel to the super luxury of the "Grand Mercedes" 600 which convinced *Car*

The 300 SEL 6.3 litre is a luxurious, leather-upholstered, air-conditioned town carriage for "the good life" which can out-accelerate (0 to 60 MPH in 6.5 seconds) and out-maneuver most anything on the road including many sports cars. (*Courtesy, Daimler-Benz*)

*& Driver* to declare that "The Mercedes-Benz 600 proved to our complete satisfaction that it is the best car in the world."

The present Mercedes line begins with the 220 and 220D cars, which may be slightly confusing to Mercedes fans who are accustomed to thinking of the 220 series as six cylinder cars. The new 220s are now fours, although the gas-engined 220 with 116 horsepower and a new rubber mounting system to dampen vibration seems to have the power and smoothness of a six. A grandson of the old 260D of 1936, the current 220D represents the top of the state-of-the-art of Diesel cars for silence, power, and overt durability. From a standpoint of pure practicality and economy the 220D must certainly be the ultimate car. Using basically the same body as the 220 series, two six-cylinder versions called the 230 and the 250 are also offered. These have 2.3 litre and 2.5 litre engines each, respectively, developing 135 HP and 150 HP.

The six-cylinder 250 mentioned above now stands at the top of the medium range of cars and should not be confused with the luxury class 250 series which was introduced in 1965. The 250S became one of the most desirable of the new generation cars and was particularly successful in the American market. They were very civilized, restrained, and highly developed machines. In a 1966 road test *Road & Track* summed up the car very well as one which "appeals to the intellect, not the libido". Presently, the same car continues as the 280S/SE, which is virtually unchanged from its successful predecessor except for the newly designed 2.8 litre six-cylinder engine which offers power and acceleration surpassing that of most American V-8s. The 280S with two twin-barrel downdraft carburetors offers 157 horsepower at 5600 RPM (although it can handle 6300 RPM), and the fuel injected 280SE puts 180 horsepower into action at 5600 RPM. A 280SEL, or long wheelbase version with extra rear seat room, is offered as a "demi-limousine". Although it shares the same fuel injected powerplant, the 300SEL is a more elite version of the semi-formal town car, coming with air suspension, leather upholstery, electric windows, and other amenities as standard equipment.

A similar sounding car, the 300SEL 6.3 litre, is, however, an entirely different breed of animal. It is a hybrid crossing

When the 250 series was introduced in 1965 it was recognized as one of the most desirable of the new generation Mercedes-Benz and was very successful in the American market. Presently the car has evolved into the 280 S/SE with the addition of a new high-torque, 2.8-litre engine which offers power and acceleration surpassing that of most American V-8s. (*Courtesy, Daimler-Benz*)

the chassis of the 300SEL with the enormous power of the 6.3 litre fuel-injected, 300-horsepower V-8 engine and transmission of the 600. The result is a curious and unique anomaly among modern cars; a sedate sedan of conservative mien which can, on demand, easily out-accelerate and out-maneuver virtually anything else on the road, including most all-out sports cars. Visually, the car can be detected from the standard 300SEL only by means of some small chrome numerals, "6.3", and by the fat Dunlop, wide-profile SP tires. But the performance is, in contemporary

holstery, electric windows, automatic transmission, and other amenities as standard equipment. (*Courtesy, Daimler-Benz*)

The current Mercedes-Benz line begins with the 220, which is now a four-cylinder car. With 116 HP and a new rubber mounting system to dampen vibration the 220 seems to have the power and smoothness of a six. (*Courtesy, Daimler-Benz*)

terminology, "something else". With a curb weight of 3890 pounds the 300SEL 6.3 litre will accelerate from zero to 60 MPH in 6.5 seconds, zero to 80 MPH in 12 seconds, and zero to 120 MPH in just over 31 seconds. Top speed is comfortably near 140 MPH. These figures, and the genuinely fabulous roadability and control that go with them, would do credit to any high grade sports machine, but for a luxurious leather-upholstered, air-conditioned town carriage intended for "the good life" they look even better. Apparently, quite a few luxury loving, affluent, sub-conscious racing drivers agreed. When the 300SEL 6.3 was introduced in 1968 at $14,000 the "copy" buyers promptly lined up and bought out the year's entire production run in short order.

A grandson of the old 260 D of 1936, the current 220 D Diesel represents the top of the state-of-the-art of Diesel car construction. From a standpoint of pure practicality and economy the 220 D must certainly be the ultimate car. (*Courtesy, Daimler-Benz*)

The "new generation" Mercedes-Benz philosophy with respect to sports cars took an interesting tack. When the 300SL and 190SL were discontinued in 1963, their successor was the 230SL, a strikingly individualistic and contemporary sports car powered by a modified version of the 220SE engine. In concept, the 230SL represented a comfortable middle ground between its two predecessors, offering more power than the little 190SL and more comfort and amenities than the austere, competition-bred 300SL. Interiors offered the thick leather seats and walnut trim of the Grand Touring machine combined with the pert, lively qualities of a small sports car. Styling incorporated the now famous high-visibility "pagoda top" which makes the 230SL design possibly unique in that it has a detachable hardtop that looks permanent. Later, the 230SL grew into the 250SL, borrowing the basic engine of the 250SE. Presently, it has evolved into the 280SL using the advanced new engine of the 280SE/300SE series. Apparently, the development has now come full circle, for the newest 280SL offers 300SL performance plus disc brakes, greater comfort, and air-conditioning.

Occasionally, rumors smoulder and flare up about a new Mercedes "super sports car" based on the powerful 600 V-8 engine. There is a good bit of precedent for such thinking in the predictable German logic of Mercedes history, and it would not be too surprising if just such a car did emerge some day. As far back as the pre-World War I 28/95, Mercedes engineers were developing a sports car out of an existing touring car, and of course Dr. Porsche's "S" cars of the twenties began as touring cars and "matured" into sports machines. More recently, the 300SL, or at least its engine, was developed from the 300 touring cars. A 600SL for the 1970's is a most intriguing thought, and one not easily dispensed with.

*Il grande signore e la grande macchina.* Singer Enzo Stuarti, an avid afficionado of fine road machinery, and his favorite Mercedes-Benz 300 SE convertible. (*Courtesy, Enzo Stuarti*)

The 600 "Grand Mercedes" is an effective answer to those who argue that "great cars" are a thing of the past. At about the time that the first new generation 220s were being introduced, Daimler-Benz engineers set to work to revive a legend, the omnipotent "Grosser Mercedes". Four years later, they unveiled what is undeniably the world's best car. The Mercedes-Benz 600 sedan is at the least an imposing automobile; but in its 246-inch-long pullman limousine version it is nothing less than intimidating. And the closer you look the more intimidating it tends to get. It does not take long to discover that the 600 Mercedes is a very great deal more than simply a big car. It is, succinctly, the very best car that Daimler-Benz can build when the cost, according to Rudolf Uhlenhaut, is of "secondary interest".

Owner John C. North II has reason to be proud of this 500K.

Since it was first shown at the Frankfort Motor Show late in 1963, the spectacular specifications of the 600 have become fairly well known. It is powered by a fuel-injected, overhead-camshaft V-8 engine of 6.3 litres (386 cubic inches) displacement which, conservatively, yields 300 horsepower at 4100 RPM and will push the 5380 pound sedan and 5800 pound limousine, respectively, at 128 MPH and 124 MPH. Acceleration, with the better part of three tons on board, is on the order of zero to 50 MPH in seven seconds. Further, a three-ton, 20½-foot limousine that handles like a small sports car is not exactly commonplace. When *Sports Car Graphic's* test driver tried the 600 over a twisting European back road he could report no better time over the same course in a well pushed 230SL. He observed that driving the 600 "really felt more like driving a 1500 cc car than a six litre, 5400 pound machine." This endearing quality can be traced to the superb suspension based upon air suspension, refinements on the swing axle, torsion bars, and telescopic shock absorbers. *Road & Track* testers compared the ride to American luxury cars and were moved to observe that "in this area (suspension) the American luxury cars fall far short as they tend to set up that great Detroit wallow on any road surface that is less than perfect." On a typical double bump which would make "most American sedans bounce wildly, the suspension of the 600 soaks it up without the least discomfort to the occupants. This is a most remarkably effective suspension system."

More superficially, the 600 is a whirling mass of wild and wonderful gadgets guaranteed to amuse and amaze. There is a central hydraulic system which acts as a sort of modern day genie-in-a-bottle, closing the doors with the flick of a finger, adjusting the seats (both horizontally and vertically), positioning the armrests and headrests, opening and closing the windows (with a silence and ease that must be

The pristine condition of the author's twelve-year-old Mercedes often fools the unknowing into believing it to be a recent model. (Perma-Tone Studios)

experienced), running the sliding roof, closing the trunk lid, and even lifting the spare tire out of its compartment for you when you need it. When the driver's door is closed and locked, from the inside or outside, it automatically locks all the other doors, the trunk lid, and the gas cap. Naturally, when a door is opened the interior lights go on, but when it is closed they *stay* on, long enough for you to find your key and put it in the ignition, thanks to a delayed action switch. The interior lighting is, in fact, quite adequate with thirteen different locations. Air conditioning vents abound all over, making it possible to produce entirely different climatic conditions in the front and in the rear of the car. For pleasanter days there is a sliding roof over the rear passenger compartment.

The interior of the 600, while incorporating all the latest Daimler-Benz safety innovations, has lost none of the old elegance. Inside is an oasis of opulence, rampant with rolled and pleated leather or luxurious velour mohair and a virtual forest of glistening burled walnut wainscotting and cabinetry. Adequate space is provided for radio, television, and telephone connections or a small bar. The rear-facing club chairs in the pullman 600 make ordinary jump seats in other limousines dreadfully utilitarian.

Less tangible than the engineering, the pleasant gadgetry, and even the obvious luxuries is the overall soothing feeling which comes from simply sitting in an unreservedly well conceived and well built automobile. It is difficult to conceive of what sort of car will come along in the future to displace the 600 Mercedes-Benz as the ultimate automobile, although something eventually will. But whatever it is, it will undoubtedly be carrying a three-pointed star.

# About the Author

Louis William Steinwedel is well known to aficionados of classic, antique and sports cars who read the national motor magazines. His articles there, always written from first-hand knowledge of his car-subjects, and with unusual charm (which adds something to automotive writing), appeal to readers who appreciate having more than nuts-and-bolts to contend with . . . the Steinwedel touch.

The author, who "batches it" in Baltimore, professes to work at the Law, but those who know him will argue the point that his heart belongs to the more romantic things of life—more to torque than to tort. Among his interests are handcrafted antique guns which he collects, and, of course, the great cars which he admires and drives when he can, and about which he will write at the drop of a Law book.

*The Mercedes-Benz Story* is Mr. Steinwedel's first book. It will not be his last. At this juncture, the point is moot whether his next will concern the great age of sports cars (foreign, of course)—or the great car of a sporting age, the Duesenberg (American, of course). Both are well beyond the dream stage—both will be Steinwedel prototypes.